HISTC
of the
HUMAN SCIENCES

Volume 1, No. 1   May 1988

CONTENTS

REVIEWS

BOOKS RECEIVED

Editorial

Someone has remarked that a science unable to forget its past is a science in difficulty. In the sociocultural sciences, however, the Cartesian advice to commence by forgetting is nothing so much as a desire always to begin afresh, unencumbered by received knowledge, older conceptual language, or an historical subject matter. One would be hard-pressed to find a more self-defeating doctrine, for knowledge of society and culture is especially inseparable from the development and historical construction of that knowledge. The role for history in the human sciences as a whole should be to investigate and clarify the relationship between our knowledge and the sources of its formation.

This quotation comes from a paper by Lawrence Scaff which is to appear in the second issue of this journal, and it captures well our intended role for *History of the Human Sciences*. But first a word about the title. The words 'human sciences' raise more problems in the English-speaking world than would their French or German equivalent. Scaff's paper is on the formation of the sociocultural sciences in Germany at the turn of the century, so the cast and the action are well known, and their stage, that of *Kulturwissenschaften*, reasonably well defined, at least in retrospect. With human sciences the case is different, and it is not enough to say we mean the English equivalent of *les sciences humaines*, or *Kultur-* or *Geistes-wissenschaften*. When we attempted to enlist support for our activities from departments within our university, one of them, while enthusiastic about the project, thought the term 'human sciences' seriously misleading for English-language academic studies, since it is traditionally used with connotations different from those we intended. But times change and so do words, and recently there has been a spectacular convergence of interest, from several disciplines, upon an area which is now widely and aptly referred to in the English-speaking world as 'the human sciences'.

'Human sciences', like the German *Geisteswissenschaften*, encompasses a number of different disciplines, including sociology, psychology, anthropology, and linguistics. Unlike 'social sciences' it suggests a critical and historical approach which transcends these specialisms and links their interests with those of philosophy, literary criticism, history, aesthetics, law, and politics. This journal will be concerned with the substantive, theoretical, and methodological achievements claimed by these disciplines, both from their own point of view and for the light they throw on the shared assumptions and preoccupations characteristic of the human sciences as a whole. It will be concerned especially with their history and foundations, in the belief that the success of studies in the human sciences can only be maintained by critical examination of current concepts and methods and their origins. The accumulation of empirical studies, while necessary, is not sufficient.

In this journal, therefore, we hope to publish work on the following overlapping themes:

1. *The history of individual disciplines and their shifting boundaries within the human sciences*

The intellectual and political arguments that surround the often tortuous formation of a new discipline (e.g. psychoanalysis, sociology, aesthetics) provide important material for the historian of the human sciences. These arguments reflect a combination of internal and external factors – internal through the responses of practitioners to the theories, methods, and findings of their colleagues, external through the encouragement or discouragement of whole disciplines, subdisciplines, methodologies, or fields of research by private and public funding agencies. In addition, much work has still to be done on interdisciplinary transactions (e.g. by borrowing concepts and metaphors from related fields, as in Stephen Bann's paper in this issue on history and its siblings), and on the establishment of hybrid disciplines – for example, the papers by Nikolas Rose, on mental testing, and Barry Richards, on Witmer's 'clinical psychology', in the next issue. The examination of boundary disputes and territorial expansion is another promising way of understanding this essentially contested field of study.

2. *The dependence on theoretical and cognitive presuppositions in the human sciences*

In the natural sciences, the construction of theoretical terms and the investigation of their interrelations has traditionally been attempted without reference to a wider cultural understanding. Such attempts are much less plausible in the human sciences, which have a more complex and problematic relationship to the way we ordinarily think about ourselves, our knowledge, our cultural and symbolic products, and our societies. A number of presuppositions inform the direction and character of various disciplinary endeavours. Some of these arise directly from everyday knowledge of the human world, others from philosophical and aesthetic reflections on both the human and natural worlds – as Anthony Pagden shows in his paper on the 'defence of civilization' in eighteenth-century social theory. The journal will publish work which clarifies these issues by viewing from a wider perspective than that of a particular discipline.

3. *The infusion of literary and aesthetic forms in the human sciences*

The recognition that a range of literary devices is involved in the work of the human sciences has been a recent and very active development. The texts of any science (and *a fortiori* the human sciences) are the work of authors writing at a definite historical moment, within a disciplinary matrix, and drawing from literary and rhetorical traditions. Such texts are written to persuade as well as to describe and explain, and this literary quality of human and natural scientific texts has a number of unexplored implications for their analysis and understanding. A variant on this is Michael Ann Holly's paper in this issue on the way Burckhardt's subject, the Italian Renaissance, determined the structure of his thought and writing. Perhaps art is itself a form of knowledge, as Norman Bryson implies in his account of realism in the paintings of Gros.

4. *The character of substantive findings in the human sciences and their institutional implications*

The findings of the human sciences are never of merely academic relevance, and the distinction between pure and applied knowledge is even hazier in these disciplines than in others. Knowledge penetrates society in a number of different ways – from the adoption of a theory of human conduct as part of an attempt to control behaviour, to a general acceptance and utilization of the products of particular disciplinary endeavours. The establishment of the 'management sciences' is a recent, and very successful, example. Many concepts first advanced as part of the technical vocabulary of the human sciences have been incorporated into lay understandings and aesthetic representations of the world.

5. *The deployment of historical resources in the human sciences*

History itself provides a paradoxical resource for the human sciences. It is both a discipline within the human sciences embraced by this journal, and a method of enquiry which contributors will wish to use, sometimes upon itself, as in the papers by Merquior and Bann. Such cognitive juggling of a piece of cultural knowledge as both a topic and a resource is a common, and perhaps inevitable, feature of the human sciences. Thus in the second issue Baldamus writes on the classification of classifications, while the historian of psychology Roger Smith asks whether the history of psychology has a subject.

Papers within the human sciences tend to fall into loose groupings, and where this occurs our policy will be to publish members of a group together. Thus the papers of the second issue will be, loosely speaking, on particular disciplines (mainly psychology and sociology), while those of the present issue are more specifically on history and historiography. These are not 'special issues', though special issues with guest editors are planned from time to time. Approximately a quarter of the space will regularly be devoted to review articles and book reviews.

History and her siblings: law, medicine and theology

STEPHEN BANN

It would be an interesting exercise to chart the development of links between the historical profession, as it has developed over the past two centuries in Europe, and the institutionalized forms of power in the modern state. At the very outset of the nineteenth century, Chateaubriand could still portray the historian as a kind of avenging angel, who would outlive and finally denounce the tyrant. Writing in the *Mercure* in 1807, he conveyed his disillusionment with Napoleon through a transparently clear classical allusion: 'When in the silence of abjection, no sound can be heard save that of the chains of the slave and the voice of the informer . . . the historian appears, entrusted with the vengeance of the nations. Nero prospers in vain, for Tacitus has already been born within the Empire.'[1] Chateaubriand's prophecy is more than a mere rhetorical gesture; indeed it can be said to convey rather precisely the relationship between the considerable power of the individual writer in the Romantic period, and the still imperfect techniques of coercion vested in the new bureaucracy of the Napoleonic state. Far into the century, this note continues to be struck, on both sides of the Channel, though Lord Acton is perhaps unique in holding steadfastly and simultaneously to the new, German-influenced, view of the historian as a member of a professionalized caste, and the conviction that only historical witness can tip the finely balanced scales of power relations in the direction of liberty for the individual in the modern state.

The picture is, up to a point, a clear and comprehensible one. In spite of Acton, the historian of the old type, vested with the moral authority of the classical tradition and heir to the Enlightenment, yields inevitably to the historians of the new type, whose authority derives from membership of a professional group which has supervised their training and admitted them to membership. In her fine study, *The Amateur and the Professional*, Philippa Levine points out the difference right from the outset when she explains her failure to deal with perhaps the most celebrated figures of British nineteenth-century historiography in her survey of the growth of the historical profession. Neither Carlyle nor Macaulay, she insists, 'was ever part of the wider historical community but found their associates and friends rather in literary and political circles of a more general kind'. Carlyle and Macaulay, who belonged to 'an older tradition of essayists and reviewers', kept their distance from the growing community of professional historians and deliberately refrained from joining the newly founded institutions (Levine 1986: 3).

Of course, there was a reason for this standoffishness. Both Carlyle and Macaulay knew their public, which far transcended that of any professionalized section, however worthy. To the extent that the historical profession distanced itself from the wider intellectual community of writers and readers, it also forfeited the right to speak directly to a mass audience, and to justify its products by the simple measure of market demand. There still remains an unresolved, although possibly fruitful, dilemma in historical scholarship: whether to continue to address the community of trained historians, or to break out decisively into the popular market which can, arguably, be captured without any loss of critical standards. I would risk a broad generalization here, in saying that the French historical profession of the present day has made the decisive breakthrough, whereas its English counterpart has been disinclined to do so. The growth in the sales of historical works in France over the last twenty years has been extraordinary, and it is even rumoured that trained historians control most of the important non-fiction lists in the major publishing houses. By contrast, British historians perhaps tend, at times of crisis, to play a different card; it is not so much their access to a mass market as their discreet and privileged right of entry to the corridors of power that carries persuasion. A recent meeting convened by British historians 'in defence of History' took place in the House of Lords, and revealed the interesting fact that there are more life peers who are professional historians than there are from any other discipline.

My analysis has admittedly been superficial up to this point. But I hope that it has served to show a real tension which underlies the development of professionalized history. From the time when the editors of the newly founded *English Historical Review* determined that their contributors should receive no payment for their articles (Levine 1986: 174), a certain sanction was given to the view that historical writing was essentially non-commercial – that it was an activity of intrinsic value whose costs should be borne, in the last resort, by the state. But this decision, which was of course simply one significant indication of the way in which the profession had started to move long before the foundation of the *E.H.R.*, entailed a possible risk. The danger is well outlined by Frederick Olafson in his broad enquiry into 'History and the Humanities', that history should present itself as 'some permanently established bureaucratic entity that is far too majestic to have to justify itself by demonstrating its continuity with wider human interests' (1979: 231–2). That group of life peers, meeting in the Lords, might well cause an unfavourable commentator to see the institution of history in Olafson's terms, however much their public pronouncements reiterated the relevance of historical research to 'wider human interests'. By contrast, the spectacle of the French historians muscling in on a burgeoning market for non-fiction might convince the expert in contemporary cultural accountancy that a need is being met, and paid for.

However, my intention is not to continue this very broad presentation of the dilemmas of history in an unfriendly world; it is to concentrate on just one aspect of the analysis of history as an institution that has come to the fore recently – significantly enough, in the adventurous publications of the French 'new historians'. Readers will perhaps have noted that in the preceding pages, the word 'profession' and its derivatives sound like a kind of litany. An article of faith for the contemporary specialist in historical research is the assumption that before 1800 there were indeed historians, but only after that date does it become possible and necessary to speak of the *professional* historian. Now, it is one thing to view that crucial development in terms of the eventual separation of the 'professional' and the 'amateur', as Dr Levine does with immense detail, bringing in the familiar antitheses between untutored enthusiasm and technical skill, between writing for a market and writing for the sake of science, which we can accept without any difficulty. But it is quite another matter to view the question of professional status as it were transversely – to ask in what respect the professionalization of history entailed a borrowing of the conventions and procedures of other existing professions. Dr Levine recognizes the existence of this question when she charts the numbers of clerics involved in historical societies and when she notes the intriguing coexistence in Stubbs of a detached, scientific ideal and a providential view of God's historical purpose. But I suggest that its full significance can only be appreciated if we adopt a very much wider time-scale, and place the issue of professionalism to the forefront.

First of all, it is necessary to recall that, if historians have only claimed professional status comparatively recently, there are professional callings which reach far back into the origins of modern Western culture. A dictionary of 1654 lists the four professions as being medicine, jurisprudence, theology, and philosophy. Of these, the first three, at any rate, have existed for many centuries within a secure institutional framework, admitting their members according to clearly defined criteria and laying claim to a monopoly, or at least a privileged awareness of a particular type of knowledge. The French historian Marc Ferro sees the development of professional medicine as offering a particularly close correlation to the professionalization of history. But his argument passes by way of a third point of identification, which is relevant both to medicine and to history. This is the administration of government by an increasingly separate and self-aware political class. Hence history can be seen to follow in the footsteps of medicine, but only to the same extent that medicine provides an administrative model for the political class, the professional politician, in the modern state. Ferro in effect begins with one hypothesis. He advances the notion that

> to make itself autonomous with regard to the power of the Prince and of ideology, the 'scientific' order has adopted modes of functioning which are similar for activities as far apart as historical analysis, political thought, the social sciences, medical research; that, confronted with power, the medical order, the scientific order and the historical order have conducted themselves in similar ways, which have resulted at the same time in the institutionalization of a profession and the establishment of a discipline. (Ferro 1985: 115)

According to this hypothesis, which is very much consonant with Acton's nineteenth-century view, the process of particularization and differentiation takes place *over against* the threat of state power. Yet Ferro actually argues a rather different point, which is that the self-defining profession provides a paradigm for the nascent political class, and in the end reveals itself to be symmetrical with state power in its offering of a knowledge to which no adequate response can be made by the private citizen. Lenin, he suggests, was fond of repeating that pure amateurs wanting to 'cure society of its ills' were in the same position as those who claimed to be able to cure a sick man 'without having studied medicine' (Ferro 1985: 115–16). Before the contemporary politician, the 'private citizen has no more right to speak than the patient has in front of his doctor'. Just like the doctor, the politician converts elementary messages of complaint ('It hurts' – 'My salary is too low') into a learned language to which he has a privileged access: what comes out is the diagnosis of a Latinate disease, or the politician's litany of rates of inflation, patterns of growth, and surplus value (Ferro 1985: 117).

Where exactly does history come into this? Ferro pictures the muse Clio 'between Marx and Dr Knock' – the latter being the doctor created by the novelist Jules Romain who saw the 'triumph of medicine' in the fact that the professional man, and not the patient, now had to make the decision as to whether the latter was well or not. He sees the fundamental analogy between professionalized medicine and history as lying, first of all, in this non-reversible flow of diagnostic knowledge – with the historian diagnosing, so to speak, the sickness of the body politic – but also in the particular kind of relationship which both professions entertain with their auxiliaries. Thus medicine purports to speak for and assimilate the findings of more specialized scientific disciplines like biochemistry, in the same way as history puts to use the auxiliary sciences of palaeography, numismatics and so on – in the same way as history would like to press into service the proliferating 'social

A MAJOR NEW JOURNAL
FROM ROUTLEDGE

HISTORY *of the* HUMAN SCIENCES

VOL 1 No 1 MAY 1988

CONTENTS

REVIEW ARTICLES

Routledge
Journals

The publication of *History of the Human Sciences* reflects a recent spectacular convergence of interest, from several disciplines, upon an area which is now widely and aptly referred to as 'the human sciences'.

'Human science' encompasses a number of different disciplines, including sociology, psychology, anthropology and linguistics. Unlike 'social science', it suggests a critical and historical approach that transcends these specialisations and links their interests with those of philosophy, literary criticism, history, aesthetics, law and politics. This journal will be concerned with the substantive, theoretical and methodological achievements claimed by these disciplines, both from their own point of view and for the light they throw on the shared assumptions and preoccupations characteristic of the human sciences as a whole. It will be concerned especially with their history and foundations, in the belief that the success of studies in the human sciences can only be maintained by critical examination of current concepts and methods and their origins.

Selected Contents
Number 2 (publication October)

Volume 1 published 1988 consists of two issues only, published in May and October.
Frequency thereafter: 3 issues per year
ISSN 0952 6951

**Routledge
Journals**

SUBSCRIPTION ORDER FORM

Individuals	Institutions
UK & ROW £25	UK & ROW £40
N. America $45	N. America $75

Please enter my subscription for *History of the Human Sciences Journal.*

I enclose a cheque/money order to the value of

£ _____ made payable to Routledge Journals.

Please send me a sample copy. ☐

Name _____

Address _____

_____

Please charge my
Access/Visa/American Express/Eurocard

Card No. _____

Expiry Date: _____

Signature _____

Please give the registered address of your credit card separately if different from that above.

Please add equivalent of £1 bank clearance charge for non-sterling cheques.
Please send to: Sally Allison,
Routledge Journals Promotion Department,
11 New Fetter Lane, London EC4P 4EE.

Routledge Journals

sciences'. Perhaps, for Ferro, the definition of a profession, as opposed to a discipline or a science, lies essentially in this fact: that the profession does not merely define its own norms, but seeks to convert adjacent findings into its own currency. Thus he quotes Michel de Certeau's comment on the historical approach: 'it sees itself as a noble speech [*une parole noble*] which obliterates the trace of its auxiliaries' (Ferro 1985: 116).

This particular aspect of the historical approach will need further discussion at a later stage. For the moment, it is worth recording, as Ferro does, that comparisons between the method of medicine and that of historiography have their own historical location in the ancient world. Polybius compared the historian's practice to that of a doctor, in the sense that both types of specialist were concerned with collecting signs, interpreting them, and arranging them in chronological order. He also suggested that the historian was capable of exercising, like the doctor, a therapeutic role; in his dealings with society, he was bound, like the politician, to offer a discourse which interpreted and validated the sense of collective purpose (Ferro 1985: 117). No doubt Polybius is consciously recalling the example of Thucydides, whose kinship with the legendary founder of medical practice, Hippocrates, has often been noted. Not only does Thucydides provide, in his famous account of the development of the plague at Athens, a superbly clear diagnosis of the stages of the terrible disease, but he also traces its insidious effects in the social and moral comportment of the citizens of Athens. Thucydides is, as one modern commentator puts it, the historian of 'pathos' as opposed to Herodotus, the historian of 'ethos'. And, in a general sense, this implies the same sort of connection between Thucydides and the present-day historian as there is between the ancient medical writer and the modern medical researcher (Parry 1972: 48).

Ferro has some further points to make about the parallels between the development of medicine and that of history in the last two centuries. He notes the decline in the prestige of general medicine, and the corresponding growth of the specialist, from the late nineteenth century onwards. Historical scholarship, and specifically the current of research associated with the *Annales* school, has taken the same path. In attempting a more and more rigorous specialization, it has retained its traditional diagnostic role, and to the extent that it also deals with the *longue durée*, it may even be said to have a limited capacity for prognosis. But any therapeutic purpose which it might have had is now deliberately kept in the background, at least in Western society, as an index of the historian's intellectual independence. In the last resort, Ferro seems to be indicting the contemporary historian for his uneasy, and probably unconscious, complicity in the unholy marriage between Marx and Dr Knock. In the early part of the twentieth century, 'the social body and the human body were invested simultaneously with the double power of medicine and politics; they were squared up, and reduced to figures and curves. . . . Well, it was just at that time, during the 1920s precisely, that the New History was created by the *Annales* school. Its programme was to use the methodology of the social sciences to promote at one and the same time economic history and the analysis of the organization of societies' (Ferro 1985: 126). Against this indictment, the claim that such specialized research is undertaken purely in the interests of knowledge, and that intellectual independence is a self-evident value, comes to seem somewhat hollow. In other words, the self-defined ethos of the professional body prevents it from appreciating precisely what, in Ferro's view, is its objective social role; it misrecognizes the relationship of knowledge to power, being unaware that the docility of the ordinary citizen before the specialist is the trait which links its procedures with those of the doctor and the politician.

Ferro's provocative analysis shows us Foucault's analysis of power relations cutting across the bows of the *Annales* school. But it does not offer many clues about the particular ways in which the historical profession has developed and refined its methods over the past two centuries. Here Paul Veyne, a French historian of the classical world, seems to go right to the mark when he traces the links between historical methodology and the controversial apparatus of jurisprudence. If there is any single principle which modern historians take as their badge of professionalism, this is the technique of *Quellenforschung*, which essentially rests on the reasoned discrimination between primary and secondary sources. So strong is the magnetism of this notion that a noted historian like Momigliano will seek to track it down even in the historiography of the ancient world, as when he commends Eusebius for incorporating documents in his historical account. Yet Paul Veyne is surely right in doubting whether the practice of Eusebius actually adds up to a 'new value attached to documents'. It can be much more convincingly represented as a literary technique which has its precedents in the period before Eusebius, and only through a kind of retrospective illusion can it be made to exhibit critical discrimination of the modern kind.

> Eusebius transcribes, not really his sources, but extracts; he compiles 'partial accounts', as he himself puts it in the first lines of his history. Enshrining precious fragments and sparing oneself the trouble of writing the history oneself by copying out one's predecessors: far from testifying to a new attitude, Eusebius confirms the 'absolute objectivity', in Renan's term, with which late Antiquity envisaged the book of history. The method of taking large extracts is already to be found in Porphyry . . . and Eusebius also practises it in his *Preparation*. (Veyne 1983: 25)

This particular dispute is, of course, not primarily concerned about which of the two historians can demonstrate the most extensive knowledge of Eusebius and his predecessors. It is about a particular mode of professional behaviour.

Momigliano is simply doing what innumerable historians of the nineteenth century did, for example, with Thucydides: he is reaching across the centuries to salute a brother, and in so doing he confirms the modern historian's confidence and self-esteem. (It is a practice slightly reminiscent of the Catholic Church's incorporation of 'virtuous pagans' – those who lived before the revelation of Christ – into the flock of the redeemed.) Veyne sees no need to make this gesture. For him, the epistemological distinctions of modern historiography have no place at all in the earlier period.

For this reason, Veyne is a particularly acute commentator on the tradition of historiography; he refuses to make a fetish of the modern critical method, and as a result he indicates how very remote its concepts are from the contemporary context of the historical account, as far as he can determine. One very telling example of his approach is provided by the French historian Estienne Pasquier, who published his *Recherches de la France* in 1560. According to G. Huppert, Pasquier circulated his manuscript among his friends before publication, and received general condemnation for his habit of giving frequent references to the sources which he was quoting. The objection to this helpful practice was that it appeared to be reminiscent of the medieval schoolmen and was in no way appropriate to a work of history. Did Pasquier really have to confirm 'what he was saying by reference to some ancient author' (Veyne 1983: 18)? If he wished to give his work authority, he would have to wait for the slow processes of time to endorse his message. After all, as Pasquier's friends asserted, the works of the ancients were not clogged up with references, and they had stood the test of time!

Veyne's example is a fascinating one, since it draws attention to an entirely credible cultural conjuncture in which the historian's system of references – so indispensable to him since the nineteenth century – seems to have appeared as slightly suspect, as a way of claiming authority which the text (*'son dire'*) did not justify. Indeed he goes on to suggest that the expectations placed on historical texts at that time must have been far more closely akin to those which we currently bring to journalism, rather than to history proper. We scarcely expect a good investigative journalist to specify his sources, in the same way as a historian. We lend credence to the journalistic text partly because we know that it can be challenged (in a rival paper, or in 'Letters to the Editor'), but also partly because we can test it for a kind of intrinsic plausibility and adequacy, which is bound up with our recognition that the journalist is himself a professional. Of course, in our own day 'journalism' is implicitly contrasted with history, and so has the connotations of a limited, ephemeral viewpoint, corrected by the historian in the long run. To register Veyne's analogy appropriately, we have to imagine the test for good journalism being applied in circumstances where that binary opposition did not yet exist.

But if Pasquier's references failed to strike his friends as germane to historical method, how did it come to pass that the citation of authorities became an inseparable part of the historian's presentation? Veyne's answer to this question is very relevant to our purposes, since he holds that the historian takes his cue from legal and theological controversy. Consistent use of references emerges, at least in the French context, in the case of historical works which are themselves implicitly of a controversial nature, like Bossuet's *Histoire des variations des Eglises protestants*; it is sustained, in Veyne's view, when the rise of the French university in the seventeenth and eighteenth centuries develops the possibility for a more formal type of controversial interchange which had previously existed only for the bar and the pulpit.

An interesting point arises here. The controversial text of history cannot have the same immediate and practical purpose as the speech at the bar (or the same redemptive purpose as the sermon from the pulpit). Even if the mode of demonstration is similar – in the sense that authorities are specifically cited – the goal is not an acquittal or a conviction, but an authoritative historical text. Hence the final 'judgement' is indefinitely suspended. As with Pasquier, the assent given by the scholarly public over a lengthy period is in the end the only legitimizing criterion. It could be argued that this is a feature which is common to historical texts over a very long period, from Thucydides and his determination to create a 'possession for all time' in his history of the Peloponnesian War, to the most sophisticated contemporary publication. But at the same time, it is surely significant that, in the period when the professional historian of modern times was emerging, this opposition be-tween the immediate pay-off and the long-term effect could be presented in terms of the different expectations placed on history and the law. In 1670, the French historian Pellisson-Fontanier announced his intention in his *Projet de l'histoire de Louis XIV* of writing 'not as a lawyer [*avocat*] but as a historian'. If Pellisson-Fontanier recognized this specific difference, and saw it as the clue to his historical project, it is also evident that historians of the following century, when disputes about the origins of French institutions acquired a strong political cast, tacitly elided the difference between historian and lawyer. A recent survey of French historiography in this period has described Moreau's *Discours sur l'histoire de France* as 'a historical defence of the monarchy, a sketch for a lawyer's brief'.[2]

I should emphasize at this point that I am not defending a trans-historical notion of 'objectivity' which was possible for Pellisson-Fontanier in the seventeenth century, but impossible for his successors in the period leading up to the French Revolution. What seems to me much more worthy of attention is the mere propinquity of the historian's function to that of the lawyer – given the controversial connotations of the system of citing authorities – and the simultaneous need for the historian to adhere to some of law's protocols, while asserting his intermittent disagreement with its objectives. It is this structure both of complicity and disavowal that seems to be implicit in the development of professional historiography, as it defines itself through its institutions and its practices. Philippa Levine's study is a mine of information on this count, particularly as regards the early development of the English Public Record Office, which she sees as having nurtured the first truly professional group of English historians. She notes that the very term 'record' was traditionally defined in the legal sense of admissibility as evidence in a court of law (Levine 1986: 101). When the Public Record Office opened its public search rooms in 1866, it applied the ruling that 'literary searchers' should be admitted gratuitously whilst 'legal searchers' should make a payment. 'It was argued that whereas the legal searcher sought record evidence for the settlement of matters of personal profit, literary applicants were indulging a scholarly principle dissociated from material gain' (Levine 1986: 105).

As Dr Levine suggests, it is worth taking up the point that the benevolent policies of the Public Record Office implied a distinction between 'legal' and 'literary' searchers; although the justification for this distinction lies in the difference between 'scholarly' objectives and those involved with 'material gain', there is no specific mention of a historical profession, entitled by its calling to have free and unimpeded access to records. However close they might have been in practice, the 'literary' applicants and the potential 'historical' applicants must be differentiated within the terms of our argument. To be classed as 'literary' was to be accredited as a member of a large and amorphous group of 'men of letters' whose activities did not have so immediate an expectation of profit as the legal searches did (though they must clearly have had *some* expectation of profit, if an eventual publication was envisaged). In order to fence off the historian's province within the broad area of scholarly publications, it was no doubt necessary to define a particular type of writing, and to perpetuate it by offering a specific type of organ for its publication. This was what transpired when the *English Historical Review* was founded in 1886. And though the journal's quite promptly introduced policy of not paying contributors was undertaken largely through financial necessity, it could also be justified as conferring a special kind of purity on the aims and achievements of the professional historians who wrote for it – a kind of *mana* which so-called scholarly journals have been content to diffuse up to the present day.

This gradually introduced division between the historical profession and the community of 'men of letters' obviously has its bearing on what I was hinting at earlier in this article, when I made the very broad comment that the French historical profession seems to have muscled in on the scene of non-fiction publishing, whilst the British historians prefer to underline their access to the corridors of power. However impressionistic this judgement may be, it is worthwhile juxtaposing it with the premiss on which Dr Levine's study is based – which is that an account of the rise of the professional historian in nineteenth-century England must omit all reference to the two writers who quite overwhelmingly influenced the historical consciousness of the Victorian public, at least in the mid-century period. To repeat Dr Levine's point 'neither was ever part of the wider historical community but found their associates and friends rather in literary and political circles of a more general kind'. Macaulay and Carlyle may have written 'great and influential historical works', but they deliberately distanced themselves from 'historical institutions' like the printing clubs and societies (Levine 1986: 3). The paradox is only an apparent one. Neither Macaulay nor Carlyle, any more than Hume or Gibbon, thought of the historian as speaking from any other ground than the central ground of literary culture, where professional barriers were inoperative. That does not mean that they were unaware of a significant difference between literature and history; indeed Macaulay spent a large part of his youthful essay on history explaining that the task of the historian was to take on and defeat Sir Walter Scott at his own game! But it does mean that they were, in a real sense, competing in the same stakes as the other literary practitioners. Correspondingly, they had little tolerance for the Rankean self-effacement before the sources which was to become a protocol of professionalized historiography. It is impossible to imagine that a contributor to the *English Historical Review* would have taken time off in a note, as Macaulay does, to label his source materials as 'nauseous balderdash' (Hale 1967: 238).

If Macaulay is the clearest possible example of a historian who scorned the disciplines of professionalism, there is a revealing case of professional history at the crossroads in the career of William Stubbs, appointed Regius Professor of History at Oxford in 1866. J. W. Burrow has spoken of Stubbs as a 'transitional figure'. On the one hand, 'in declaring his intention of avoiding political preaching, [he] was paying tribute to a growing sense of professional responsibility, and proclaiming his dedication, in a manner later to become fashionable and even mandatory, to the cause of pure truth'. Yet if he disclaimed the kind of prophetic role which his predecessors had adopted, he was still convinced that the study of history was, to take his own words, 'thoroughly religious' (Burrow 1981: 100). The answer to this apparent paradox lies in the fact that, for Stubbs as indeed for Ranke, the scrupulous observance of the new techniques of *Quellenforschung* helped to create a type of historical writing which retraced the workings of the Divine Providence, without arrogating to itself the role of superior judgement which belonged only to God. Burrow puts the matter effectively:

> Judgement for him meant judicious appraisal, a fine sense of the complexity of things, and even a proper respect for the mysteriousness of the workings of the superintending Divine Providence in which he so firmly believed. Philosophers of history seemed to him to wish to

circumscribe by supposed laws the historical discretion of the Almighty. Generalisation is an aspect of our imperfection. We cannot study history without it, but God, being omniscient – it is plainly suggested – is a nominalist. (Burrow 1981: 132)

Yet this excursion into the intellectual history of the nineteenth century diverts us to a certain extent from the main purpose of this article, which is to look at the particular ways in which history has borrowed or assumed the protocols of other professional practices. Veyne's contention is that history borrows its system of references from the controversial practices of law and theology. In the light of this claim, the attitudes of Stubbs and his contemporaries seem particularly revealing. The university historians of the mid-century found themselves initially in the same boat, whether they liked it or not, with the academic lawyers. At Cambridge, a Moral Sciences Tripos examination was established in 1848 to include political economy, moral philosophy, jurisprudence, English law, and history. In 1867, jurisprudence and history were simultaneously ejected from the tripos to form a short-lived Law and History Tripos before, in 1873, the History Tripos was eventually established as a separate entity (Levine 1986: 136). A similar pattern can be observed at Oxford, where once again a forced marriage with jurisprudence took place before the independence of the School of History was established in 1871. Just as in the reading rooms of the Public Record Office, historians and lawyers were participating in the same institution, and using the same documentary materials. How could the historians achieve and justify their independence? Stubbs's strategy is surely the exemplary one in these circumstances, since he places in the foreground the necessity of 'judgement', yet withdraws from the term precisely those connotations which are appropriate to the legal sense of the term. Historians are not advocates, pleading for summary judgement. Their patient scrutiny of the documents of the case will never result in a condemnation or an acquittal, in the final sense, since that role belongs to God alone.

So Stubbs, Regius Professor of History and future Bishop of Chester, raises insistently the final question of this article, which is concerned specifically with the clerical profession and its links with the nascent historical profession. On the broadest level, it is obvious that clerics did not have an unblemished reputation for fair and unbiased enquiry, at least from the eighteenth century onwards. Indeed they could be said to have become a byword for special pleading, to the exclusion of objectivity and truth. Montesquieu can think of no better way of stigmatizing Voltaire's capacity as a historian than by comparing him to a monk; Voltaire, he claims, 'would never write a good history: he is like the monks who do not write for the sake of the subject they are dealing with, but for the glory of their order. Voltaire writes on behalf of his convent.'[3] It is possible to argue that monks were, in fact, among the most

scrupulous of eighteenth-century historians, since the Benedictine congrega-
tion of St Maur was compiling outstanding documentary collections during
the period, with a fine disregard for the interests of the convent. But the
achievement of the Benedictines was recognized only in the next century,
when a more sophisticated historical profession was able to salute their simple
scholarship and put it to further use. More typical of the eighteenth century,
no doubt, were the hordes of English clerics who assailed Gibbon with
vituperative pamphlets after the publication of his *Decline and Fall of the
Roman Empire*, and were dealt a series of devastating blows by the provoked
historian in his *Vindication*. Gibbon leaves us in little doubt that these
pamphleteer historians were writing, if not for their convents, at least for their
colleges and for the hope of future benefices; and in at least one case, it seems
as though one of Gibbon's assailants received notable preferment for his
efforts against the depreciator of the Early Christian Church.

Up to a point, we can settle the question of the link between historiography
and the clerical profession on these fairly simple and obvious grounds. The
majority of those concerning themselves with historical research in late-
eighteenth- and early-nineteenth-century England were clerics. However,
clerics did not, and could not, live by historical research and had to look out
for ecclesiastical preferment. Therefore it seems reasonable to suppose that
the interests of historical research would be sacrificed, if it came to a choice, to
the need for prudent churchmanship and ephemeral partisanship. Such a
pattern does in fact fit, so it would appear, even the rare cases where a cleric
was in fact able to derive a modest income from historical lectures and
research. There is the example of Edward Nares, rector of Biddenden in Kent.
Obliged as he was to support a wife who was the daughter of a duke (and with
whom he had eloped), Nares secured the interest of the Prime Minister, Lord
Liverpool, and gained the Regius Chair of History at Oxford from 1813. But
his lecturing experiences were disappointing, and he was soon tempted to
resign. What caused him to stay the course was the assurance that 'being a
Crown Appointment, it could only prove a step to something better'.[4] So, in
1827, he put forward his candidature for the more lucrative Chair of Divinity.
But he was late in the field and had to content himself with hanging on to the
Chair of History.

In this particular case, the 'professing' of history seems to have been
scarcely more than a useful sideline in a clerical career, swiftly to be
abandoned if more solid preferment could be obtained. But there is another,
more serious point to be made about the links between history and theology,
which reaches beyond their institutional form to the most central issues of
intellectual method. If the development of historiography in the eighteenth
and nineteenth centuries entailed close parallels with the legal paradigm, we
can also say that it involved a similar, though more uneasy, relationship with
the theological paradigm. Law covertly lent its controversial apparatus, but

theology was apt to make itself manifest as the 'last instance' – the *ultima ratio* against which historical research had to be viewed.

A fascinating example can be taken from the great age of English antiquarianism. William Stukeley deserves acknowledgement for his pioneering work in the field of archaeology, of which the most well-known aspect was his fieldwork at Avebury. Stukeley toiled for many years over the interpretation of what he found at Avebury and at length in 1730 he was ready to reveal his conclusions to a friend: 'The form of that stupendous work . . . is a picture of the Deity, more particularly of the Trinity, but most particularly what they anciently called the Father and the Word, who created all things' (Piggott 1985: 104). Stukeley's biographer, Stuart Piggott, puzzles over the pioneering archaeologist's desire to 'combat the deists from an unexpected quarter' by making this remarkable pattern plain: indeed he finds it particularly odd that Stukeley had abandoned his 'excellent intentions' of an earlier date, when he was planning 'an objective work on stone circles and British Celtic prehistory' (Piggott 1985: 106). Not only has Stukeley taken leave of his objectivity, but he has also, in a sense, repudiated the more scholarly habits of an earlier age. 'We have travelled a long way from the accurate scholarship of the Restoration historians, in the last decade of which tradition Stukeley began his work.'

However justified such a comment may be, it can also be seen in some sense as a reflection of our own, post-eighteenth-century viewpoint. So well established is our own sense of the achievements of professionalized historiography, that its emergence seems to have been subject to an irreversible law, and such reversals and regressions as the case of Stukeley brings to the fore, are apt to seem strange and paradoxical. But to view the matter in this way is in fact to succumb to a proleptic illusion. Even at the height of the nineteenth century, English historians did not set store on 'accurate scholarship' to the exclusion of all else; indeed 'accurate scholarship' was, in a certain sense, established only in so far as it was *permitted* by a particular religious world-view. Philippa Levine rightly infers that the so-called empirical stance of nineteenth-century historians like Stubbs, with its apparent championing of detailed reconstruction as an end in itself, was in fact the product of a particular ideology. 'In rejecting – or more accurately, not considering – the materialist interpretation proposed by Marx, historians were asserting their adherence to a historical universe presided over ultimately by Providence' (Levine 1986: 169). From such historians as Ranke and Guizot in the early part of the century to those of Stubbs's own generation, the notion of Providence enabled the diligent researchers to forego controversy, in the confidence that any particular nugget of fact would be compatible with a divine purpose which could never be revealed as a whole. In much the same way as St Augustine spared later Christian historians the impossible task of justifying God's severity to the earthly empire of Rome, so the providential view of history sanctioned the evacuation of all theories and all partisanship of an overt nature from the infinitely particularized text of the reality of the past.

Yet to contrast 'accurate scholarship' with a theological or providential view of history in this way is to set up an asymptotic series. The two concepts are not precise enough to be compared or contrasted, at least on the level of the historical text itself. Where does one end and the other begin? I suggest that it may be more revealing to think of the whole process of historical reconstruction, particularly in the eighteenth- and nineteenth-century cases with which we have been concerned, as the process of attaining a particular *viewpoint*. In other words, mastery of the historical materials is equated with setting them out in an intelligible order which can be termed *perspectival*. Note that in the case of Stukeley's investigations at Avebury his fieldwork could only be interpreted through careful sketches of the circles as seen from above. It was this 'bird's eye' view that enabled him to reach – long after he first began to sketch the circles – the conclusion that they formed in effect 'a picture of the Deity'. Stukeley's exercise corresponds to the Vitruvian exercise of 'ichnography', which is the use of rule and compass to trace forms as if on the ground. But the technical process, informed by his fieldwork at (and below) ground level, leads inexorably to the possibility of taking a commanding view of the whole site; and in that act of viewing, the image of Deity is ultimately revealed. It is as if Stukeley was able to coincide, in this final act of seeing, with the viewpoint of the Christian Deity seeing his image inscribed upon the earth.

This metaphor of perspectival ordering becomes even more explicit, though in an ostensibly secularized form, in the writings of Macaulay. And it is never more plainly demonstrated than in his confutation of the unfortunate Edward Nares. Macaulay begins his devastating criticism of the Burleigh Memoirs, edited by the Regius Professor, with an evocation of the bulk and weight of the edition: 'It weighs sixty pounds avoirdupois' (Macaulay 1883: 220). But this indictment of the excessive size of the edition becomes more precise when he stigmatizes Nares's failings in quasi-pictorial terms: 'Of the rules of historical perspective, he has not the faintest notion. There is neither foreground nor background in his delineation.' Macaulay's final point against Nares is consistent, on the metaphorical level, with the twin indictment that the edition is too bulky and heavy, and that its materials are devoid of perspectival ordering. Dr Nares is accused of being 'so utterly incompetent to arrange the materials which he has collected that he might as well have left them in their original repositories' (Macaulay 1883: 221). In its structure, this highly revealing argument by the young Macaulay shows that the failings of Nares belong at exactly the opposite end of the spectrum from the proud boastings of Stukeley. Where Stukeley has, by a powerful act of sublimation, transformed the brute earth of Avebury into a figure of the Deity, Nares has extracted his materials from the Burleigh archives only to meet the complaint that they might as well have remained there. A kind of gravitational pull drags them back into the undifferentiated, literally invisible mass from which their editor aspired to rescue them. That Macaulay really viewed the uncoordinated materials of libraries and archives with a disgust which was almost physical is attested by his further comment on the 'nauseous balderdash' that he was obliged to consult for his social history. 'I have been forced to descend even lower, if possible, in search of materials', writes the intrepid historian – almost as if he wished to fix in our minds an image of historical research as the Harrowing of Hell (Hale 1967: 238).

Yet neither Stukeley nor Macaulay gives as powerful an image of the irresistible force of sublimation which raises base materials to the level of true historical vision as does Lord Acton. For Acton, indeed, the task is Herculean: to win victory, Hercules must lift his rival Antaeus from the earth on which he stands. In his letter to the contributors to the *Cambridge Modern History*, which began publication in 1902, the year of his own death, Acton viewed international co-operation between scholars as the only means of bringing about this great feat. But as a reward for their labours, he held out the tempting prospect that all further historical research would be rendered unnecessary by the definitive and comprehensive nature of the enterprise. 'As archives are meant to be explored, and are not meant to be printed, we approach the final stage in the conditions of historical learning' (Stern 1970: 247). Quoting from his original proposal for the collective work to the Syndics of the Cambridge University Press, Acton paints a devastating picture of the *selva oscura* in which the 'honest student' is obliged at present to find his direction: he 'has to hew his own way through multitudinous transactions, periodicals, and official publications, where it is difficult to sweep the horizon or to keep abreast'. This vivid evocation of a limited viewpoint is then triumphantly transcended in a passage where Acton simultaneously liberates the student of the future from the labyrinth of the archives and from the inconvenience of belonging to one place and time:

> By Universal History I understand that which is distinct from the combined history of all countries, which is not a rope of sand, but a continuous development, and is not a burden on the memory, but an illumination of the soul. It moves in a succession to which the nations are subsidiary. Their story will be told, not for their own sake, but in reference and subordination to a higher series, according to the time and the degree in which they contribute to the common fortunes of mankind. (Stern 1970: 249).

Acton's 'mobile army of metaphors' (to adapt the Nietzschean phrase) is here drawn up on parade. By 'Universal History' is understood the pursuit of brightness rather than darkness, the light rather than the heavy, the high rather than the low, and that which is teleologically directed rather than randomly occurrent. And if Acton does not, like Stukeley, picture the Deity inscribed upon the earth after this feast of metaphysical distinctions, he uses a striking image to make concrete his abandonment of the ethnocentric point of view. 'Contributors will understand that we are established, not under the Meridian of Greenwich, but in Long. 30 W.' The point from which Europe is merely a set of co-ordinates on the surface of the spinning globe is fleetingly envisaged.

This brief investigation into history's relations with its siblings thus comes full circle. Medicine helps us to appreciate the relationship of professionalized history to political power, but offers few precise parallels apart from the kinship of diagnostic (and maybe therapeutic) aims. Law is more intricately involved in the self-realization of the historical profession: it shares with history the controversial method, and the issue of judgement, so that historians have had to fight hard to dissociate themselves from its institutional embrace. Theology enters on many more levels. If so many historians have derived their bread and butter from the service of the Church, the possible conflict of loyalties was not settled by the advent of the strictly professional caste, in the nineteenth century. Chateaubriand's avenging angel still haunts the discourse of Lord Acton, though he has sheathed his sword and simply directs towards the earth his piercing, non-partisan point of view. There is an active metaphysical residue in the combination of terms which Acton uses to underline the transcendence of 'Universal History'. Surely it is this persisting feature which Michel de Certeau detects when he claims that history sees itself as a *parole noble* 'which obliterates the trace of its auxiliaries'? What we must ask about history's nobility today is whether, at this stage, it can be anything more than a life peerage.

University of Kent

NOTES

1 Chateaubriand later described his article in the *Mercure* as a covert protest against the emperor's execution of the Bourbon Duc d'Enghien, on 21 March 1804. He recounts that the emperor reacted violently to this evocation of the avenging role of the historian. 'Does Chateaubriand think that I am an idiot, that I don't understand him . . . I'll have him cut down on the steps of the Tuileries.' See Chateaubriand, *Memoirs* (Harmondsworth: Penguin, 1965), 245–7, 254–5.
2 Baker (1985) draws an interesting contrast between Pellisson-Fontanier in the previous century and Moreau's need to argue a specific historical case (153, 163).
3 Quoted in Chateaubriand, *Genié du Christianisme* (Paris: Garnier-Flammarion, 1966), I, 445.
4 See G. Cecil White (1903), 227.

BIBLIOGRAPHY

Baker, Keith Michael (1985) 'Memory and practice: politics and the representation of the past in eighteenth-century France', *Representations* 11: 134–64.

Burrow, J. W. (1981) *A Liberal Descent*, Cambridge: Cambridge University Press.

Ferro, Marc (1985) *L'Histoire sous surveillance* ['History under surveillance'], Paris: Calmann-Levy.

Hale, J. R. (ed.) (1967) *The Evolution of British Historiography*, London: Macmillan.

Levine, Philippa (1986) *The Amateur and the Professional*, Cambridge: Cambridge University Press.

Macaulay, Lord (1883) *Critical and Historical Essays*, London: Longman.

Olafson, Frederick A. (1979) *The Dialectic of Action*, Chicago: University of Chicago Press.

Parry, Adam (1972) 'Thucydides' historical perspective', *Yale Classical Studies* 22: 47–61.

Piggott, Stuart (1985) *William Stukeley*, London: Thames & Hudson.

Stern, Fritz (ed.) (1970) *The Varieties of History*, London: Macmillan.

Veyne, Paul (1983) *Les Grecs ont-ils cru à leurs mythes?* ['Did the Greeks believe in their myths?'], Paris: Le Seuil.

White, G. Cecil (1903) *A Versatile Professor – Reminiscences of the Rev. Edward Nares*, London: R. Brimley Johnson.

Philosophy of history: thoughts on a possible revival

J. G. MERQUIOR

What I mean by 'philosophy of history' is not the theory of history in its general sense. Rather, philosophy of history denotes here just a species of the genus 'theory of history'. Since Hegel we emphatically know that the theory of history has two distinct, though not, of course, unrelated objects: the historical process itself, and the proper knowledge thereof – the theory, not of substantive history, but of historiography. Now if, paying homage to Droysen, we call the theory of historical inquiry 'historics' (Droysen 1974), then we might say that not all theory of history is historics. Besides historics, the theory of history comprehends a theory of the historical process. Let us call this other species of the genus theory of history 'philosophy of history', even if this goes against the grain of the contemporary literature on the subject, at least in English.

For mainstream Anglo-Saxon philosophy of history since the war has been but a historics with a Kantian vengeance. Its leitmotiv is: how is proper historical knowledge possible? Thus what in Droysen was mainly a job of *description* – describing the interpretation of the past – became a problem of *constitution*: what are the epistemological grounds, and constraints, of our grasp of history? To illustrate the point with famous theses, is historical knowledge in the critical sense a matter of bringing particulars under covering laws, as Hempel (1959) thinks, or does it rather partake of the nature of narratives, as Gallie (1964) or Ricoeur (1983) holds, not to speak of tropes, as Hayden White (1973) has brilliantly suggested? Obviously, such queries reach beyond the humbler issues of Droysen's historics; so much so, that one feels tempted to call this kind of theory of history *metahistorics*.

Yet the queries of metahistorics, important though they are, are often raised in a spirit unconcerned with the meaning of history itself. Worse still, they are often pursued in a cast of mind bent on implying the illegitimacy of any philosophy of history in the substantive sense. Whilst metahistorics is acknowledged as the sole 'critical' branch of the theory of history, philosophy of history gets short shrift as a spurious 'speculative' lucubration.

There is nowadays a growing dissatisfaction with this state of affairs.[1] Naturally few would want to ditch metahistorics as a critical enterprise. But many begin to suspect that banning philosophy of history as such as an incorrigibly speculative exercise might well be an attitude far less critical than it seems. Hence the pressing question: can we make an honest woman of philosophy of history? Can it be reclaimed from wanton speculation into a reasonably analytical theoretical structure?

The main stumbling block, it would appear, is the traditional association between philosophy of history and *historicism*. Since Popper, English-speaking readers have little excuse for mixing up historicism and *historism*. Taking historism to be the view that things should always be considered in terms of their historical context or development, Popper equated historicism with logics of history couched in pseudo-laws. Historicism is the doctrine of historical laws.

Historism, on the other hand, need not be confined to its generic above-mentioned sense. Indeed in the great German tradition of Historismus it meant something else, namely, an obsession with the *uniqueness* of historical phenomena or of historical contexts. As one of its chief interpreters, Friedrich Meinecke, liked to stress, in the footsteps of Goethe: *individuum est ineffabile*. Meinecke's contemporary Ernst Troeltsch made a point of defining historism as a German response to Western rationalism, whose roots he saw in natural law theory.[2] Historism, from romantic historians like Ranke to epistemologists like Dilthey, and hence to post-war theorists like Troeltsch (1922) and Meinecke (1936), repeatedly suffered from acute nomophobia: its historical individuals shunned all subsumption under universal laws, single or combined. In fact historist units themselves were often wholes but never universals – whereas historicisms spoke of history in the singular, historisms focused on histories, in the plural.

In the inter-war period, influential upholders of historism such as Croce, Meinecke, and Troeltsch were rightly perceived as distinguished historians themselves, unlike most classical historicists, who were philosophers, not acclaimed historians. Thus while historical reality seemed to give the lie to the myth of progress entertained by nineteenth-century historicisms, histori-ography itself helped to discredit historicism in favour of historism. How-ever, it would be grossly unfair to blame the *Zeitgeist*, or professional self-esteem, for the fall of historicism. The doctrine of historical laws fell on its own accord. In particular, it proved unable to bear the brunt of several lines of criticism. Each of them is so well known that I shall content myself with the barest of reminders.[3]

First, as the young Croce realized at the turn of the century, during the so-called 'crisis of Marxism' debate, we have no proper model of historical determinism. At bottom, therefore, the assertion of 'historical laws', even in materialist garb, amounts to little more than metaphysics, hard to swallow in the eyes of critical knowledge.

Second, even if there was a decent canon of historical determinism, historical prediction would remain impossible. As famously noticed by Popper, at the very least some historical events are in principle unforeseeable, for, as some developments depend on the growth of knowledge, it is impossible to predict them, since one of their conditions remains unknown to us. Therefore an Oedipus effect seriously harms the historicist claim.

Third, historicisms tend to be chiliastic: they generally assert a redemptive end of history vastly superior, as a whole, to all past epochs. Now by embracing such notions of an end of history, historiosophies like classical Marxism end up by deducing the reality of historical process from an *idea* thereof – and by so doing they slip into a modern version of the old and fallacious ontological argument about God: they deduce existence from essence. Once again, with historicism, philosophy of history degrades itself into dubious metaphysics. (This criticism, made by Troeltsch in his youthful essay on 'metaphysical philosophy of history', was to be renewed in our own time by Raymond Aron.)[4]

Finally, it has been claimed (notably by Sir Isaiah Berlin, 1954) that historicisms, by asserting historical determinism, do away with the meaning of responsible human action. Historical determinism is unproved; but, if real, it would run against the ethics of freedom. Such is the gist of Berlin's Tolstoyan objection against the idea of historical inevitability. More recently, in the wake of Leo Strauss's fierce antihistoricism, historicism, seen as the dissolution of being into time, has been deemed the source of nihilism. To put it briefly: historicism is not just silly – it is also ugly.

Note that in all four criticisms there is an underlying assumption: that historicism is, and has to be, deterministic and necessitarian. All such criticisms assume, for example, deterministic readings of Marx and necessitarian readings of Hegel. Now while the former is still hard to refute, the latter is not exactly acknowledged by some thought-provoking modern studies of Hegel.[5] Moreover, even apart from the interpretive fortunes of these thinkers, historicism in general is not bound to be equated with historical determinism. Historicism is and will always be a theory of the meaning of history but it is not necessarily a theory of historical laws. For value and meaning can certainly be found in history as a whole even without a demonstration of a pervasive historical necessity in the causal sense.[6]

Much that was demolished under the name of historicism was actually a half-caricature, or at least just a possible form of it. Furthermore, the onslaught against historicism soon became burdened with a general, yet scarcely critical, revulsion against historicity as such, both in its historist and historicist images. Several trends of thought of wide influence after 1945 bear witness to this. To take philosophy first: from Husserl to Wittgenstein, key thinkers sounded definitely atemporal. The 'pure descriptions' of phenomenology acted as a vacuum cleaner on the historical dimensions of their objects. Heidegger explicitly located his lofty history of Being, its eclipses and disclosures, well above the dust and noise of actual history. Wittgenstein's life-forms and language games often seem innocent of time and change. Meanwhile Jung invited Western thought to bathe in the lustral waters of timeless archetypes, Mircea Eliade pitted the wisdom of myth against the 'terror of history', and Leo Strauss preached a return to ancient natural law at the expense of history and all historisms. As for most modern art and literature, they unabashedly embraced what Eliot and Hermann Broch described as the big virtue of Joyce: the 'mythical method', a symbolic structure at a far remove from the previous realist mimesis, fraught with history as it was.

Thus in the high culture of the history-weary, post-bellum West, almost nothing remained of that 'historical fever' once denounced by Nietzsche as a sign of decadence. No wonder a Benedetto Croce had to end his life by holding on – to no avail – to a passionate defence of the historical perspective, bombarded from all quarters with the accusation of having so undermined moral standards as to make room for the fascist furies. Even those lines of thought most committed to resisting the fascist syndrome did not fare better when it comes to abiding by history. For instance, as Herbert Schnädelbach shrewdly points out, the Frankfurt school polemics against Heidegger's 'fundamental ontology' should not be allowed to disguise the fact that both sides used ahistorical substructures to interpret man and society – and I cannot disagree with Schnädelbach (1984: 65) when he refuses to acknowledge the Frankfurtian theme of the dialectic of Enlightenment as anything like a genuine historical model of cultural evolution.

By 1960, achronism ruled supreme. Those who blame structuralism for having abolished the historical sense do not know what they are saying: for structuralism was patently a completion, rather than a start, of the antihistory rage. The true novelty, in structuralist chronophobia, was just its aggressive methodological stance. Unlike most other de-historizing modes, structuralism offered a recipe: it enjoined us to envisage culture as a language. In olden times the jurists of the historical school also indulged in 'organic' analogies between law and language. But already by the mid-nineteenth century the great Rudolph von Jhering warned that in actual fact law resembles language very little, for while language generally undergoes few sharp conflicts and changes, with the legal framework of modern society it is the other way round. The protracted, majestic pace of change in linguistic structures has no counterpart in the much quicker evolution of law and culture – yet structuralism tends to blur the difference.[7]

As for the quarrel of structuralism with *historiography*, it requires, for our purposes, practically no comment. After all, as the doyen of historians of history, Arnaldo Momigliano (1975), reminded us in the teeth of the structuralist vogue, it is simply untrue that history-writing is ever prone to be besotted by diachrony. From Fustel de Coulanges to Mommsen and from the *Annales* school to Fernand Braudel, path-breaking advances in historiography have often been able to overcome the limitations of a strictly diachronic rendering of the past. As Hermínio Martins (in Rex 1974) has indicated, the arbitrary character of the historians' code, so criticized by Lévi-Strauss in the famous final chapter of *The Savage Mind*, is by no means a shortcoming peculiar to history: rather, it constitutes a problem of description attendant on some kinds of knowledge not even restricted to social science (e.g. the chronological codes of history are no more arbitrary than the topographical codes of geography).

With the Nietzschean bearings of poststructuralism the anti-history rage continues unabated. Foucault annexed history to philosophy. Nobody yet knows for sure which of the two came out more damaged in the process, history or philosophy. But one thing is pretty certain: the caesural thinking (if I may borrow, once again, Herminio Martins's apt phrase) that sustains Foucault's construal of the history of modern culture starkly *aestheticizes* the historical record. As for the surviving high priest of poststructuralism, Jacques Derrida, suffice it to recall how, in the third section of his book *Positions* (1972), history – the thing as well as the knowledge – is flippantly indicted for its alleged tendency to be 'repressive' by means of stealthy 'stabilizations' of meaning. Poor history – the Straussians berated it for dissolving being; now the deconstructionists scold it for freezing meaning.

Ironically, however, much of what today's conventional wisdom refuses to the good old historicisms of the Romantic and Victorian ages, the systems of Hegel, Comte, or Marx, seems to be readily granted in the guise of prevalent *cryptohistoricisms*. The very *Kulturpessimismus* rife amidst the humanist intelligentsia mirrors historicist determinism – only this time progress leads to evil and vulgarity instead of enhancing the level of civility and civilization. The Frankfurtians were masters in this gloomy progressivism. No wonder Adorno, their leading prophet of doom, wrote a sympathetic essay on Spengler, the historicist who was also the arch-cultural pessimist of the age. And there is a still more widespread cryptohistoricism of the antihistoricist mind: the blind cult of progress within avant-garde art, i.e. the naive ideal of progressive experiments in the modernist tradition. Here, too, we have a historicism *qui n'ose pas dire son nom* – and unlike the cryptodeterminism of *Kulturpessimismus*, its myth of progress is entertained with relish, not regret.

However, the persistence of historicist elements, in a detached and debased state, in the humanist consciousness says more against the latter than in favour of historicism. In order to recover a sense of the intellectual legitimacy of historicism much more is needed. In particular, we would begin to tread firmer ground if we could spot para-historicist elements in the very structure of historical consciousness itself. Now our historical sense cannot help being comparative – but, whenever it compares us with the past, ours or alien, it is bound to find roots of modernity. To a large extent, to experience an awareness of history means to recognize the past as a vector of the modern, of that kind of culture – ours – for which the sense of history, as well as of *other* histories, is an essential attribute.

Therefore we might say that our very self-understanding as modern men, in a world where modern culture became 'planetary', contains a strong ingredient of historicism. A few diagnoses of modernity, the work of Ernest Gellner, for example, focus precisely on the moral and cognitive situation of modern man as the denizen of a techno-industrial world radically new in the history of mankind.

Nevertheless, for all its radical novelty, modern culture evinces, in its main components, many a source and root harking back to the past, both Western and non-Western. Gellner's powerful sociology of modernity, centred as it is in the sharp break of *modernization*, does not analyse such germs of the modern. But the fruitful revamping of historical sociology, in the work of Perry Anderson (1983), John A. Hall (1985) or Michael Mann (1986), has been eliciting such civilizational genetics, equally illuminated by some historico-anthropological studies (e.g. Jack Goody 1983; Alan Macfarlane 1978).

The new historical sociology represents the nearest modern heir to that 'philosophical history' spawned by the Enlightenment in justification of commercial society and bourgeois values (John Hall explicitly recognizes such an ancestry at the threshold of his fine new book, *Powers and Liberties*, whose subtitle reads, Weber-wise, 'The causes and consequences of the rise of the West'). But of course it chiefly provides the principle of a reborn philosophy of history with a retrospective insight, a kind of food for thought in terms of conjectural histories whose lessons (as in Weber's famous battle of Salamis example) act as a foil that enhances the meaning of the actual evolution of civilizational patterns. As for earning the right to a *prospective* glance – that modicum, neither of wild guess nor formal forecast, but of reasoned consideration of tangible trends and plausible outcomes – we must look elsewhere – and where else, but to the (self) interpretation of our present condition, as modern or modernizing societies?

In the *Historik* of Droysen (1974; originally published in 1858), the historical consciousness knows that it has a twofold object: it understands-through-research the past, and it apprehends itself. It follows that the historical consciousness is well aware of its own historicity. Yet this implies what Michel Foucault, discussing Kant's celebrated pamphlet on the Enlightenment, felicitously described as a sagittal relation to the present.[8] Now such living relationship with the present was the very point of Hegel's grand philosophy of history. George Dennis O'Brien has rightly characterized Hegel's philosophy of history as pre-eminently a history of moments, or steps, in historical consciousness.[9] But what should also be stressed, and is by now well established thanks to the labours of Hegel scholars like Manfred Riedel, is that the whole construction was geared to a bold vindication of modern society.

The natural advantage of the historicist perspective over historist empathy hinges precisely upon this visual link with the present. While the glory of historism is the ability to avoid anachronism by a sustained effort at identification with the past, historicism alone, in one way or another, can relate the meaning of the past to the vital concerns of the present. This – and not a precarious rationalist or determinist scaffolding – constitutes the most precious legacy of Hegel and his progeny.

Historicism in this broad sense is the pith and marrow of philosophy of history. And it is more than obvious that historicism, however qualified, is a statement about history, not just about historiography. Those who, like Nathan Rotenstreich, protest against the narrowness of the current diet of metahistorics, and call for the rekindling of philosophy of history in the classical mode of a theory of history able to cope with both process and politics, do not seem to be in the wrong (Rotenstreich 1976; especially 90, 132, 139, and 151).

At any rate I strongly suspect that the discrediting of historicism *per se*, and not just of its outmoded versions, in our time has less to do with epistemological qualms than with an ideological climate. To put it simply, historicism succumbed to the assault of *Kulturkritik* – the chief mood in the philosophical scene throughout the last quarter of a century. To be sure, the ebbing away of historicist philosophies of history was already visible much earlier than that. Writing before the First World War, Troeltsch could remark that all three kinds of philosophy of history were intellectually in the cold: traditional Christian theodicy, the Enlightenment's 'philosophical history', and Hegelianism. However, it might be said that, to a large measure, all these forms of philosophy of history had fallen into abeyance because their rationale – the reasoned defence of modernity – had become a matter of course to progressive liberal minds like Troeltsch himself. In other words: historicism was out because its message had won.

Naturally ready-made historicisms, such as the cheap Hegelianism of mid-century Germany, which tried to dictate to history in the land of the greatest historians, well deserved the scorn of historians and historian-theorists. With such intellectual aberration in mind Burckhardt once described historicism as a strange animal, a 'centaur on the edge of the forest of historical studies'. Nevertheless, Burckhardt himself was not above contributing to cryptohistoricism, as in his ominous intimations about the primacy of power over culture in the age of mass society. Already, a creeping *Kulturpessimismus* was tipping the scales against historicism – and the reasons for it were far from being strictly scientific.[10]

Nowadays, I submit, the centaur can ride again. Of course its trot has to be far more cautious than in Hegel's time, if only in view of the obligation to take into account the manifold output of serious social science. But a substantive philosophy of history, soberly assessing the direction and results of historical evolution, can hardly go on being forbidden or disparaged as a subject unfit for rational analysis. What is more, the prolonged absence of such a branch of philosophy is beginning to look like a failure of intellectual nerve. Indeed a proper substantive philosophy of history would manage to cater both for legitimate intellectual curiosity and for badly needed cultural stamina.

NOTES

1 For a particularly cogent illustration, see Rotenstreich (1976).
2 Troeltsch (1922); there is an Italian translation by Giuseppe Cantillo of chapters 1 and 2 (Naples: Guida, 1985).
3 Croce (1914). Italian original, Palermo: 1900.
4 cf. the perceptive analysis of Aron's position in Mesure (1984).
5 For the state of contemporary Hegel scholarship, see MacIntyre (1972); and Inwood (1985).
6 Significantly, it is with precisely similar considerations that W. H. Dray closes his entry on philosophy of history for the *Encyclopaedia of Philosophy* (Dray, 1967).
7 On this point, see the criticism by Anderson (1983: 44–5); and my comments in Merquior (1986a: 199–209).
8 An excerpt from Foucault's course at the College de France on Kant and the Enlightenment was published by *Magazine Littéraire* 207 (May 1984). I discuss it in Merquior (1985: 149–52).
9 cf. his chapter on Hegel's *Philosophy of History* in Inwood (1985), as well as his book *Hegel on Reason and History* (1975).
10 The collapse, in the hands of *Kulturkritik*, of a theory of process in most self-appointed 'critical' social theory of philosophical origins since the war is one of the main themes of my book, *Western Marxism* (1986).

BIBLIOGRAPHY

Anderson, Perry (1983) *In the Tracks of Historical Materialism*, London: Verso, 44–5.
Berlin, Isaiah (1954) 'Historical inevitability', reprinted in I. Berlin (1969) *Four Essays on Liberty*, Oxford: Oxford University Press.
Croce, Benedetto (1914) *Historical Materialism and the Economics of Karl Marx*, New York.

Derrida, Jacques (1972) *Positions*, Paris: Les Éditions de Minuit.

Dray, W. H. (1967) 'Philosophy of history', in Paul Edwards (ed.), *Encyclopaedia of Philosophy*, London: Macmillan.

Droysen, Johann Gustav (1974) *Gundriss der Historik*, Darmstadt. Originally published in 1858.

Gallie, W. P. (1964) *Philosophy and the Historical Understanding*, London: Chatto & Windus.

Goody, J. R. (1983) *The Development of the Family and Marriage in Europe*, Cambridge: Cambridge University Press.

Hall, J. A. (1985) *Powers and Liberties: The causes and consequences of the rise of the West*, Oxford: Basil Blackwell.

Hempel, Carl G. (1959) 'The function of general laws in history', in Patrick Gardiner (ed.), *Theories of History*, New York: New York Free Press.

Inwood, M. (ed.) (1985) *Hegel*, Oxford: Oxford University Press.

Macfarlane, A. (1978) *The Origins of English Individualism: The family, property and social transition*, Oxford: Basil Blackwell.

MacIntyre, Alasdair (ed.) (1972) *Hegel: A Collection of Critical Essays*, New York: Doubleday.

Mann, M. (1986) *The Sources of Social Power*, Cambridge: Cambridge University Press.

Merquior, J. G. (1985) *Foucault*, London: Fontana.

Merquior, J. G. (1986a) *From Prague to Paris: A Critique of Structuralist and Post-Structuralist Thought*, London: Verso.

Merquior, J. G. (1986b) *Western Marxism*, London: Collins.

Mesure, Sylvie (1984) *Raymond Aron et la Raison Historique*, Paris: Vrin.

Momigliano, Arnaldo (1975) *Essays in Ancient and Modern Historiography*, Oxford: Oxford University Press.

O'Brien, George Dennis (1975) *Hegel on Reason and History*, Chicago: Chicago University Press.

O'Brien, George Dennis (1985) 'Philosophy of history', in M. Inwood (ed.), *Hegel*, Oxford: Oxford University Press.

Popper, Karl R. (1957) *The Poverty of Historicism*, London: Routledge & Kegan Paul.

Rex, John (ed.) (1974) *Approaches to Sociology*, London: Routledge & Kegan Paul.

Ricoeur, Paul (1983) *Temps et Récit*, Paris: Seuil.

Rotenstreich, Nathan (1976) *Philosophy, History and Politics: Studies in Contemporary English Philosophy of History*, The Hague: Nijhoff.

Schnädelbach, Herbert (1984) *Philosophy in Germany 1831–1933*, Cambridge: Cambridge University Press.

Troeltsch, Ernst (1922) *Der Historismus und seine Probleme*, Tübingen: Mohr.

White, Hayden (1973) *Metahistory*, Baltimore: Johns Hopkins University Press.

The 'defence of civilization' in eighteenth-century social theory

ANTHONY PAGDEN

I

Today we all live in cultures. Some of these are highly local, most are discrete. We speak of 'political cultures' and 'popular cultures', in very much the same contexts as we speak of the 'culture of Bali' or the 'culture of the Hopi'. We do not, on the whole, speak of civilizations except in the past tense. For civilization, unlike culture, suggests both a process (that of civilizing) and comparative evaluation. It describes a state, social, political, cultural, aesthetic – even moral and physical – which is held to be the optimum condition for all mankind, and this involves the implicit claim that only the civilized can know what it is to be 'civilized'.

'Civil', 'civility', and 'to civilize' are terms which were already in wide general use by the mid-sixteenth century. They all derive from *civitas* and they all, in the first instance, indicate those values associated with the life lived in cities, in ordered communities with recognized social structures and fixed locations, lives which, to use the corresponding set of Greek derivatives, were also 'politic', and thus also 'polite' and – the word most often used by the Scots – *polished*. By the mid-eighteenth century, however, these terms had become, largely if not exclusively, attached to a set of formal behavioural characteristics, to what were called broadly 'manners'. 'Polite' and 'civil' had thus come to acquire much the same range of references as they possess today. They still described those qualities which separated social man from the savage; but they were now far more heavily freighted with the sense of what criteria might be used to distinguish between individuals *within* civil society. That 'civility' had already begun to lose its former antithetical clarity is suggested by the fact that when Johnson refused to include the word 'civilization' in his dictionary, Boswell protested, 'with great deference to him', that he thought *civilization* from *to civilize* better in the sense opposed to *barbarity* than *civility*' (quoted in Dampierre 1960: 334). The rapid acceptance of the term was also part of the transformation and extension of a conceptual vocabulary for social theory which is characteristic of the human sciences in the Enlightenment. Just as Montesquieu had successfully established a distinction between 'savages' as men in the state of nature who live in 'small dispersed groups which, for some particular reason, are unable to group together' (*ne peuvent pas se réunir*) and 'barbarians' who have entered some kind of society (*qui peuvent se réunir*) but who are still at a very low level of civility (Montesquieu 1951: XVIII, 11), so it was now possible to distinguish between cultural and technological progress on the one hand, and the evolution of the finer shades of social behaviour on the other. 'Civilization' thus became an important concept in the language of those whose social theory constituted a refutation of the claims that men had become morally corrupted by society, and that the ideal human community must approximate, as far as it was able, to the state of nature. In particular 'civilization' was used as challenge to the image set out in Rousseau's *Discours sur les sciences et les arts* (1750) and the *Discours sur l'origine et les fondements de l'inégalité* (1754) of a world in which human achievement and human inequality, though perhaps inescapable, were none the less both highly undesirable and contrary to man's true nature. The opposition to Rousseau and the 'defence of civilization' has received relatively little attention. This is partly because the social imagination of the 'Newton of the moral world', as Kant called him, seemed far to exceed that of any of his critics, and because so many of his opponents seem to have taken Judith Shklar's point that if, as Rousseau claimed, his state of nature had never had, nor could ever have, any real existence, it must be merely a moral fable, a strategy for arousing the reader's moral recognition (Shklar 1986: 8–10). But there is a substantial body of literature, by no means intellectually insignificant, which began with the premiss that Rousseau's vision constituted a radical utopian alternative to civil society, and that such a vision was grounded in the claim that there did exist (or certainly had once existed) an imaginable state in which man was at one with nature and in which the inequalities which were the principal feature of civilized societies were unknown. Most of Rousseau's critics, or the critics of what was believed to be Rousseau's position, were political economists. They were committed to the view that contemporary commercial society was the highest condition to which man could aspire and that such a society was a possible outcome – possible for all peoples everywhere – of a determinate, intelligible, and, to some degree, controllable, historical process. It is with this literature that I shall be concerned in this article. The coverage is necessarily scanty and the argument, such as it is, inconclusive. My claim is merely that we will be in a better position to understand the project which went under the name of 'the human sciences' if we understand the place which the contrasting notions of 'nature' and 'civilization' played in them.[1] These, then, are some preliminary notes towards such an understanding.

II

The word 'civilization' itself seems to have been coined by Mirabeau *père* in 1756 (see Starobinski 1983: 14),[2] although in his usage it varies hardly at all from the common sense of 'civility'. It was, he said, the 'softening of customs, urbanity, politeness, and the spread of understanding so that the niceties are observed'. Such a definition made it possible for him, in his attempt to establish religion as the only lasting check on man's naturally destructive passions, to speak of 'the barbarity of our civilization' and of civilization as masking the true moral and political virtue.

But as Emile Benveniste has pointed out, 'civilization' differs crucially from 'civility' in that its *-ation* ending indicates the presence of an agent, and of an agent who is purely human. This last point, together with the fact that the term had for long had a legal significance (the transfer of a case from a criminal to a civil court) located it immediately in a discourse which, as Benveniste says, was '*résolument non théologique*' (Benveniste 1966: 307). It was, therefore, far better suited than 'civility' had been to describe the outcome of a continuous process – that of 'civilizing' – and was rapidly absorbed into the vocabulary of the new 'philosophical' and 'natural' history of human society. Civilization was, as Benjamin Constant later observed, primarily the outcome of co-operative action, of a continual process to which men are committed by the nature of their intelligence 'which is unable to remain still' (Constant 1815: 146). Men in the state of nature, because the demands of their physical environment are so great, are capable only of very low levels of co-operation. Montesquieu's savages were savage precisely because the degree of sociability attained by the primitive warrior horde was insufficient to allow for the development of the 'arts and sciences'. As Boswell had seen, 'civilization' described the antithesis to this condition far better than 'civility' would have done.

Why these terms – 'civilization', 'civility', 'barbarism', 'savage' – should have come to acquire during the Enlightenment, and beyond, the pre-eminence they did within this particular set of socio-anthropological concerns, requires, however, some preliminary historical explanation.

III

By the beginning of the eighteenth century the Aristotelian, natural law explanations for the origin and evolution of human societies which had previously been used to guarantee the primacy of the European moral and social order had ceased to have any real explanatory force. Europeans had also acquired a very substantial body of information about non-European cultures which had helped to further destabilize the view that there could be anything more than a minimal law of nature applicable to all cultures everywhere. If any degree of moral certainty was to be rescued from the sceptic's claim that there simply were no moral facts which could be established beyond any reasonable doubt, then it had to be both independent of scholastic natural law arguments and sustained by enough sociology to cope with the inescapable facts of the diversity of human social behaviour. The great seventeenth-century, Protestant, natural law theorists, Puffendorf and Grotius, had recognized this. But their solution had been to limit the ethical code to the minimal claim that what contributed to the survival of the individual (what was *utile*) must also, by any argument from design, be right (*honestum*) (see Tuck 1987: 99–119).

Grotian minimal moral philosophy may have secured the pass – or one pass – against the sceptics, but it did nothing to explain why men should choose to behave in so many different ways, nor did it contribute towards a comparative evaluation of different cultures. One attempt to provide a new answer to these questions was, of course *De l'esprit des lois*. But Montesquieu's typologies, and his reliance on a revised Polybian climatology, did not go far enough in explaining change. For some, at least, of Montesquieu's heirs it seemed obvious that 'civilization' could only be explained, and defended against attack, through a radical revision of the image of man's relationship to nature.

At the most fundamental level the rejection of Rousseau's moral vision involved the claims of a simple evolutionary psychology. The human species, claimed Condorcet (1793: 330) *must* be subject to a process of constant and irreversible improvement through 'the steady growth of the intellectual and physical faculties' simply because that is its innate disposition. As with the child so with the race as a whole. The pursuit of knowledge is, argued Adam Ferguson (1792: I, 206), 'no less an exigency of the mind than the means of subsistence and accommodation are an exigency of mere animal life'.

Intellectual progress, what Condorcet (1793: 57) called 'this need of ideas or new sensations, the first mover of the progress of the human spirit', generated increasingly complex sets of human needs. These, as the conjectural historians understood, increased exponentially as they were satisfied, and as they grew, so, of course, they changed. Civilization, as the Neapolitan Francesantonio Grimaldi observed, in his *Reflessioni sopra l'ineguaglianza tra gli uomini* of 1799, was the process by which the '*sentimenti naturali e simpatici*' and even the physiognomy of men were radically altered by the increased satisfaction, and thus the ever-shifting nature of their needs. Since it allows for the proliferation of satisfiable needs, civilization also produces a great variety among its members. There was, claimed the Milanese Gianrinaldo Carli (1794a) whose *Lettere americane* of 1780 offered one of the most compelling analyses of an actual 'primitive' society, no discernible continuity over time within even a single individual, let alone an entire community. Halley, he said, was not the same man when he fell in love with Mary Tooke in 1682 as he was when he observed his comet in 1680. Nor, he claimed, was the Newton who wrote commentaries on the book of the Apocalypse the same man who discovered the laws of gravity (Carli 1794a: XI, 169). The numbing sameness which Grimaldi (1958: V, 562) perceived among savages, their supposed oneness with nature which he scorned Diderot for admiring, was merely the consequence of their willingness to accept the immediate impulse to survival as sufficient. They thus all became alike, each one adopting 'a mask which makes him like his fellow'. The *varietas rerum* which previous commentators had struggled so hard to explain away and which, in the eyes of men like Carli and Grimaldi, the savage world had eliminated in the interests of survival, simply was the substance of the human condition.

Grimaldi's image of the mask of sameness haunted the champions of the civilized world. For they were all acutely aware that the continual process of amelioration, and hence of liberation, of enlightenment, could always be blocked and as rapidly reversed. As Benjamin Constant (1967: 41–2) in his unfinished *De la perfectibilité de l'espèce humaine* bitterly observed, 'a physical calamity, a new religion, the invasion by barbarians or a few centuries of oppression could carry away all that has raised up, all that has ennobled our species. . . . In vain then would one speak of enlightenment, or liberty or philosophy.' Constant, of course, had seen the pluralistic vision of the Enlightenment overrun first by the Terror and then by the rise of Napoleon (Fontana: 1985). But even so optimistic a pre-Revolutionary writer as Condorcet (to whose *Esquisse* Constant's own treatise is heavily indebted) could construe the history of human societies as, at one level, the history of persistent attempts, sometimes by false beliefs, more often by the will of those who seek power over others, Condorcet's (1793: 336) 'tyrants, priests and hypocrites', to obstruct the natural flow of knowledge. 'All nations', wrote Raynal (1781: X, 27), 'swing from barbarism to civility [*l'état policie*] and from civility back to barbarism.'[3] But however strong these forces might be, and the champions of civilizations were not inclined to underestimate them, they must eventually crumble before the far stronger, because natural, forces of 'enlightenment'.

The process which Constant (1815: 95) called the '*égale répartition des lumières*' is ultimately inescapable. Sooner or later the cultures of the uncivilized will vanish just as the barbarisms of the European 'Gothic Ages' had vanished in their turn. Once the European colonists have shed their own shackles of un-reason they will, proclaimed Condorcet (1793: 335–7), 'civilize the savage races which have hitherto occupied such vast countries, or make them disappear even without conquest' for they, the peoples of America, Africa, and Asia, 'seem to be waiting only to be civilized and to receive from us the means to be so, and find brothers among the Europeans to become their friends and disciples'.

This insistence on illumination, on man's innate drive for an understanding which must inevitably lead to an ever-increasing sociability, demanded a radical revision of most current accounts – Rousseau's in particular – of the origins of human society. In the first place it greatly reduced the role given to individual legislators and to moments of sudden and irreversible transformation. For, Constant (1815: 90–4) argued, the kind of societies where it was possible for individual legislators and founding fathers to have had any measurable impact must have been ones in which the sum total of knowledge was very small, too small, indeed, to be regarded as significantly different from the 'barbarian' communities which had preceded them. Nostalgia, and the inherent instability of even the most civilized community, meant that the primitive yearnings for a single man to represent the age, and around whom 'all the forces will group themselves', were hard to resist. But no matter how deep our potential for barbarism may be, the civilizations we actually inhabit are, he claimed, simply too complex to have been anything other than exercises in co-operation. No one, protested Simon Linguet (1767: 221), one of Rousseau's most excitable critics, could be expected to accept as a plausible historical account, the Ciceronian claim that the origin of human society was to be found in the acts of supremely gifted first legislators. To have been capable of such deeds they would have had to have been 'celestial intelligences rather than men'. Then they would have needed to be in possession of an instrument – language – which must itself be a social artefact. And it is clearly absurd to suppose that these early men would be in a position to respond to the rhetorical claims of a Solon or a Lycurgus unless they already possessed the sentiments necessary for understanding them. 'One cannot claim', he concluded, 'that society is the effect of a sentiment of which it itself is the cause' (1767: 208–9). Men, in short, must have been capable of a high degree of sociability from the moment they first appeared on the planet. As Carli (1794b: XIX, 143) observed in his eulogy of Inca society, there was no evidence from anywhere in the world to show that man had ever lived a solitary language-less existence. Even the most primitive of peoples lived in bands held together by speech. To claim that language was an invention was to deny to man the power of communication which even animals possessed, for language is to man only what barking is to dogs, the 'signs by which they communicate their thoughts', and without which he would not have been able to survive at all.

The history of man's move towards '*l'état actuel de la civilisation*' was, for Constant, as for the political economists, in particular Smith and Filangieri, who preceded him, a history of a move away from the social values of primitive warrior bands, with their emphasis on honour and personal valour, to the impersonal world of the commercial society. War and commerce, said

Constant, are both means to a single end, 'that of possessing what one desires', but whereas war is '*l'impulsion sauvage*', commerce is '*le calcul civilisé*'. Within such communities communication – which, of course, shares a common semantic origin with commerce – determines the economic and political relationship between individuals, not force. The commercial society operates through credit and as credit, said Constant (1815: 7–11), 'is subject to opinion; force is useless'.

The philosophical history of civilization was, then, a history of progressive complexity and progressive refinement which followed from the free expression of those faculties which men possess only as members of a community. For the political economists, the insistence on a continuous historical past together with the refusal to engage in vain conjecture not only eliminated founding fathers and first legislators, it also did away with any real or useful distinction between nature and culture. 'Art itself', said Ferguson (1966: 6), 'is natural to man.' He is 'destined from the first age of his being to invent and to contrive'. The psychological model for the history of irreversible human progress had always been the life of the human individual. 'Not only the individual', wrote Ferguson, 'advances from infancy to manhood, but the species itself from rudeness to civilization.' But it was difficult to align this with the idea that the pre-social condition of men had been one in which they were, in Ferguson's words (1966: 2), 'possessed of mere animal sensibility, without any exercise of the faculties that render them superior to brutes, without any political union, without any means of explaining their sentiments'.

For Ferguson, Millar, and Smith, as for such men as Linguet, Gaetano, Filangieri, Grimaldi, Constant, and Carli, the classical 'state of nature' could, therefore, only be a simple fiction composed of 'wild suppositions' and 'fruitless inquiries' which, as Ferguson noted, were generally devised *ex post facto* to satisfy 'the desire of laying the foundation of a favourite system, or a fond expectation, perhaps, that we may be able to penetrate the secrets of nature'. Men, real men, had always been distinct, superior, and endowed with the capacity for natural improvement. What Ferguson listed as man's 'disposition to friendship or enmity, his reason, his use of language and articulate sounds' are attributes of the self; they 'are to be retained in his description, as the wing and the paw are in the eagle and the lion' (1966: 3).

As Linguet pointed out, the advocates of the state of nature from Puffendorf to Rousseau had persistently dodged the issue of whether they thought that state to have had a real existence or not. And if not, if indeed the state of nature was merely an instructive fantasy, a moral strategy, then it could be of no conceptual value for the theorist of civilization who, since he could be only a natural historian 'obliged', in Ferguson's words, 'to collect facts, not to offer conjectures', could not simply, as Rousseau claimed he could, 'put the facts aside'.

If the state of nature had indeed never had any existence in real historical time then it could never be of any use even as a thought-experiment (Hont 1987: 256–7). No man, claimed Carli (1794b: 105–6), could be compelled to any kind of moral understanding through the contemplation of a 'romance' about a condition which was wholly alien to our nature as men. Man, as Adam Smith said bluntly (1976: II, ii, 3, 85), 'who can subsist only in society was fitted by nature to that situation for which he was made'.

If the state of nature could be shown, both theoretically and empirically, to be a simple fiction, if human societies were the consequence of a natural uninterrupted growth of which the final product was something termed 'civilization', then it must also be the case that the inequalities present in all civil societies must, *pace* Rousseau, be natural ones. The seeming equality of savage society, or even of Rousseau's Alpine villages, was an illusion. Equality in ignorance, sloth, and abject poverty was mere bestiality. The only true equality was the equality of the enlightened co-operation which could be achieved only through civilization. All men might indeed be born equal; but the moral and intellectual status of the child was hardly relevant. It was what he, or she, became that mattered. The skills of the inventor and the artist, said Ferguson, depended on the toil of the mechanic. In savage societies such distinctions do not, as European travellers tirelessly remarked, exist. The savage possesses an undivided personality and, in Ferguson's words, 'acts from his talents in the highest station which human society can offer' (1966: 186). Only in barbarous societies, as Smith insisted, could the same man be a producer, a statesman, a judge, and a warrior (see Hont and Ignatieff 1983:7). Such equality could survive only at a very low level of technical development. In any civilized society there must be a marked difference between the arts and the professions, between, in Ferguson's terms, the statesman and 'the tools he employs' (1966: 183). For Smith the loss of the undivided personality, the creation of the division of labour and with it of property and of social inequality was an inescapable feature of the commercial society. Inequality was not, of course, desirable in itself; but, as his famous analogy between the condition of the African chieftain and the European pauper made clear, the only possible society of equals was not the community of semi-angelic beings of Rousseau's imagination, but merely one in which all men lived equally miserably.

IV

All the arguments in defence of civilization I have mentioned so far were based upon one or another kind of conjectural history. They were remarkably persuasive, partly, at least, because they were grounded in a large measure of sociological and ethnographical data, which dispensed with any natural law argument based upon 'innate ideas', the main prop of scholastic discussions on the subject. But the history, despite the insistence of its authors upon the certainty of their data, remained conjectural. No one could *know* what the origins of society had been, and no sociology based on historical projection could escape the charge levelled at it by the biologists that it might itself be proved false at any moment by the discovery of new data or by future events. There was, of course, another set of explanations for the human *diversitas rerum* which the philosophical histories had largely obscured. There had always been those – Bodin, Montesquieu, and Ferguson among them – who were prepared to argue that the differences between the various races of the world at any one point could only be ascribed to a set of innate characteristics operating in response to environmental conditions. The trouble with climatology of this kind was that ultimately it relied upon some weak version of classical faculty psychology which, in the end, came back to belief in innate ideas. And this, although d'Alembert came finally to accept Montesquieu's climatology as the only sound scientific basis for explaining cultural difference and Ferguson devoted a considerable amount of space to the possible influence of climates, had little appeal to most eighteenth-century social theorists, firmly wedded, as they were, to a Lockean sensationalist psychology. But if climate and situation would not do, not all were convinced that some kind of biological explanation was entirely unavailable. Even Carli had been prepared to argue that the habit of leadership, the unequal distribution of property, even the aesthetic inequalities displayed by the art of Asia, Africa, America and Europe might all correspond at some level to man's status *qua* animal (Carli 1794b: 175–85). The significant *rupture* with the more firmly sociological modes of explanation came, however, at the beginning of the nineteenth century. The growth of physical anthropology and the continuing debates over the nature of the great apes made it intellectually respectable to raise, in another and radically more deterministic language, the doubts, which had been lost sight of in the late sixteenth century with the demise of the theory of natural slavery, as to whether the genus 'humanity' might not prove on examination to contain more than one species.[4] The effect of this, and the possibility of the need, which is evident in most of the French writings on the subject, to find an irrefutable, hence scientific, argument with which to oppose the abolitionists, and, during the Restoration, to undermine all claims that a social revolution could bring an immediate change in the distribution of status within human societies, led to the revival of biological explanations for the rise and distribution of 'civilization'. For Lamarck (1809: I, 4; see also Barsanti 1983: 174–5), for whom there was a relationship amounting to interdependence between the 'moral' and the 'physical', and whose psychology was almost simplistically Lockean, civilization could simply be described as a condition of advanced sensational complexity. In the state of nature all men must be equal because all are equally brutish. There is simply nothing for their intelligences to operate on, and reason, like any other faculty, will develop only if it is used. The degree of an individual's intelligence will very much depend on what he or she does. But what he or she does will, in the first instance, be the consequence of a natural disposition. There then comes into being, he wrote, 'the real existence of a scale relative to the intelligence of the individuals of the human species' (Lamarck 1830: 327). It was this scale, he claimed, which was the first cause of the division of labour and not, as both Smith and Rousseau, with different ends in view, had supposed, the other way about. Only those who have extended leisure will be able to develop their mental capacities to the full. Those who labour will, of necessity, be made or will remain brutish, and, in a pre-industrial society, it was clear that there had to be a helot class so that the others should be free to enjoy their *otium*. By grounding this distinction, not, as all social theorists from Aristotle to Smith had done, in education but in what he called an 'organic phenomenon', Lamarck (1830: 291–2) attempted to make the process irreversible. For man there could be no condition other than that of civilization, of a world divided between those who consumed and those who produced.

Lamarck's argument for a biology of civilization exists only in outline. But one of his successors, Jules Joseph Virey, best-known perhaps for his involvement with the case of the wild boy of Aveyron, attempted, in his *Histoire naturelle du genre humain* of 1824 and a lecture delivered to the Académie de médecine in 1841 on the physiological causes of civilization, to provide a more thoroughgoing account of the biological mechanism of civilization and a legitimation of the inequalities it necessarily involved. Arguments for a natural equality of the kind put forward by Rousseau, must, he claimed, lead directly to the collapse of the civilized world. Since for Virey (1824: II, 69) man's empire over his fellow was merely a special case of his domination over other species, Rousseau's 'natural equality' between men would logically require that man abandon his domination over animals. The natural inequality between the races derives from the obvious and observable facts that the species was divided into two distinct groups: the 'blacks' – which meant all Africans, Americans, and Asians – and the 'whites' which included all Caucasians (Virey 1824: I, 436–8). The latter have already attained 'a more or less perfect level of civilization'. The others, however, never arrive at anything other than a 'constantly imperfect civilization'. The reason for this may be found in the fact, which, so he believed, few had previously noted (although it is, of course, a feature of Rousseau's account of the deleterious effects of the social process), that sociability in men is the same process as domesticity in animals – the dogs of savages were, he claimed, less docile than the dogs of civil men – for like domesticity sociability is a process of 'interior contraction' (Virey 1841: VI, 402–5). The results are physiologically evident.

Both domestic animals and civilized men have white flesh, untamed animals and uncivilized men have dark flesh. The implication of this was that refinement, the civilities which Mirabeau had seen as masking the true virtues of civil society, were in fact constitutive of it. We must, said Virey, overthrow that old and pernicious notion that delicacy leads to decay. The reverse is true. 'Even among those savages in South America', he wrote, repeating much older stereotypes of the 'Patagonians', 'where the sexes mingle without distinction of parentage and where fathers delight in corrupting their own children' all are valiant and robust. What they clearly are not is 'civilized'. True, his concept of 'delicacy' is ambiguous since it precludes sensuality and *'les peuples donnés aux plaisirs'* and it is typified by *'les hommes austères des pays froids'* (Virey 1824: I, xii–xvi). But it is equally clear the older virtues of the Roman republic – and of Revolutionary France – translate out not as the civic virtues which for an earlier generation seem to have made commercial society, and hence 'civilization', possible but as the signs of inescapably savage communities. Virey's socio-biology, deterministic and anti-historical, led him to revise arguments for natural inequality which had lain dormant for over a hundred years. He even attempted to inject new life into a modified version of Aristotle's theory of natural slavery and many of his conclusions were not unlike those which some of the apologists for the Spanish domination of America had come up with two hundred years previously, although theirs were more generally psychological than directly biological. It might, he said, seem unjust to some that there are races – the 'blacks' – who had been singled out to serve others, 'but is it any more unjust for the lion to devour the gazelle?' (Virey 1824: II, 67–70). Without an abundant supply of labour – without slavery – European civilization would not have been possible. The sceptical challenge which had dominated the human sciences for so long had been swept away. The answer to the question 'What is right?' was now being given in terms neither of a natural law theory nor of an historical empiricism but in the supposed biological, and hence 'scientific' and unchallengeable, composition of the species.

Virey's biological racism was not an isolated case and, for the Romantics and their heirs, it came to constitute the dominant features of a social theory of civilization: an insistence on the immutability of the inherited order, the claim to be a science of human conduct, above all an unfailing belief in progress and the superiority of technology over all the other 'arts'. What emerged from the Romantic critique of this image of the optimal state for man was, of course, the term we now tend to substitute for civilization: namely 'culture'. For Nietzsche, civilization was indeed precisely what Virey had declared it to be – 'the ages of the domestication of man'. But it was, as it had been for Rousseau, a domestication which had been forced upon him, which was 'intolerant of the most audacious and brilliant minds' and had atrophied his better self.

Civilization, he concluded, 'means something else than culture, something which is perhaps the reverse of culture'.[5]

King's College, Cambridge

NOTES

1 There have, however, been a number of studies on the linguistic history of the term, the most comprehensive of which is perhaps Moras (1930). But see also Starobinski (1983), Gusdorf (1971: 310–48), Beneton (1975), and for a slightly later period, Lochmore (1935).
2 Emile Benveniste claimed the possibility of a prior usage in Ferguson's unpublished manuscripts. See Benveniste (1966: 343).
3 Raynal uses *l'état policie* and *civilisation* as synonyms.
4 See, for example, Prichard (1814).
5 'Aus dem Nachlass der Achtziger jahre', quoted in Starobinski (1983: 43).

BIBLIOGRAPHY

Barsanti, G. (1983) *La mappa della vita* ('The Map of Life'), Naples: Guida Editori.

Beneton, P. (1975) *Histoire des mots: culture et civilisation*, Paris.

Benveniste, E. (1966) 'Civilisation – contribution à l'histoire du mot' ('Civilization – a contribution to the history of the word'), *Problèmes de linguistique générale* ('Problems in general linguistics'), Paris.

Carli, G. (1794a) *Delle lettere americane* [1780] ('The American Letters') in *Opere*, Milan, XI.

Carli, G. (1794b) *Della diseguaglianza fra gli uomini* [1792] ('On the inequality among men') in *Opere*, Milan, XIX.

Condorcet, M.-J., marquis de (1793) *Esquisse d'un tableau historique des progrès de l'esprit humain* ('Outline of an historical account of the progress of the human spirit'), Paris.

Constant, B. (1815) *De l'esprit de conquête et de l'usurpation dans leurs rapports avec la civilisation européenne* ('On the spirit of conquest and usurpation and their relationship with European civilization'), Paris.

Constant, B. (1822) *Commentaire sur l'ouvrage de Filangieri* ('Commentary on the work of Filangieri'), vol. V of *Oeuvres de Filangieri*, Paris.

Constant, B. (1967) *De la perfectibilité de l'espèce humaine* [1829] ('On the perfectability of the human species') ed. Pierre Deguise, Paris.

Dampierre, E. de (1960) 'Note sur "culture" et "civilisation"' ('A note on the words "culture" and "civilization"'), *Comparative Studies in Society and History* 3: 328–40.

Ferguson, A. (1792) *Principles of moral and political science*, Edinburgh.

Ferguson, A. (1966) *An essay on the history of civil society*, ed. Duncan Forbes, Edinburgh: Edinburgh University Press.

Fontana, B. (1985) 'The shaping of modern liberty: commerce and civilisation in the writings of Benjamin Constant', *Annales Benjamin Constant* 5: 3–5.

Grimaldi, F. (1958) *Riflessioni sopra l'ineguaglianza tra gli uomini* [1779–1780] ('Reflections on the inequality between men') in *Illuministi Italiane*, ed. F. Venturi, Milan-Naples: Riccardo Riccardi editore, Vol. V.

Gusdorf, G. (1971) *Les Principes de la pensée au siècle des lumières*, Paris, Payot: 310–48.

Hont, I. (1987) 'The language of sociability and commerce: Samuel Puffendorf and the theoretical foundations of the "Four-Stages Theory"', in Anthony Pagden (ed.), *The Languages of Political Theory in Early-Modern Europe*, Cambridge: Cambridge University Press, 253–76.

Hont, I. and Ignatieff, M. (1983) 'Needs and justice in the *Wealth of Nations*: an introductory essay', in I. Hont and M. Ignatieff (eds.), *Wealth and Virtue, the Shaping of Political Economy in the Scottish Enlightenment*, Cambridge: Cambridge University Press, 1–44.

Lamarck, J. de (1809) *Philosophie zoologique, ou exposition des considérations relatives à l'histoire naturelle des animaux* ('Zoological philosophy, or some considerations regarding the natural history of animals'), Paris.

Lamarck, J. de (1830) *Système analytique des connaissances positives de l'homme* ('An analytical system of the positive knowledge of man'), Paris.

Linguet, S. (1767) *Théorie des loix civiles, ou principes fondamentaux de la société* ('A theory of civil law, or the fundamental principles of society'), London.

Lochmore, R. A. (1935) *History of the Idea of Civilization in France (1830–1870)*, Bonn.

Montesquieu, Charles de Secondat, baron de (1951) *De l'esprit des lois* ('The spirit of the laws') in *Oeuvres complètes*, ed. Roger Caillois, Paris: Bibliothèque de la Pléiade.

Moras, J. (1930) *Usprung und Entwicklung des Begriffs der Zivilisation in Frankreich (1756–1830)*, Hamburg.

Prichard, J. (1814) *Researches into the Physical History of Man*, London.

Raynal, G. (1781) *Histoire philosophique et politique des établissements et du commerce des Européens dans les deux Indes* ('Philosophical and political history of the settlements and commerce of the Europeans in the two Indies'), Geneva.

Shklar, J. (1986) *Men and Citizens, a study of Rousseau's social theory*, Cambridge: Cambridge University Press.

Smith, A. (1976) *The Theory of Moral Sentiments* [1759], ed. D. D. Raphael and A. L. Macfie, Oxford: Oxford University Press.

Starobinski, J. (1983) 'Le mot civilisation' ('The word civilization'), *Temps de la réflexion* 4: 13–51.

Tuck, R. (1987) 'The "modern" theory of natural law', in Anthony Pagden (ed.), *The Languages of Political Theory in Early-Modern Europe*, Cambridge: Cambridge University Press, 99–119.

Virey, J. J. (1824) *Histoire naturelle du genre humain* ('A natural history of the human species'), Paris.

Virey, J. J. (1841) 'Des causes physiologiques de la sociabilité chez les animaux et de la civilisation dans les hommes' ('On the physiological causes of sociability among animals and civilization among men'), *Bulletin de l'académie de médecine* (Paris) 6: 402–5.

Burckhardt and the ideology of the past

MICHAEL ANN HOLLY

As a young man, Jacob Burckhardt was predisposed to melancholy. A student of two historians of daunting reputation, Leopold von Ranke and J. G. Droysen, as well as the imposing historian of art, Franz Kugler, he felt temperamentally unsuited to the prevailing modes of nineteenth-century German historiography. The positivism and political bent of Ranke's school interested but did not enchant him, and he claimed to be repelled by Hegel's metaphysical explanations of the historical process. 'I feel at times', he said as a young man in a letter to a friend,

> as though I were already standing in the evening light, as though nothing much were to come of me. . . . I think that a man of my age can rarely have experienced such a vivid sense of the insignificance and frailty of human things, in so far as they relate merely to the individual. But my respect for the universal, for the spirit of nations and of the past, increases correspondingly. . . . Pictures, *Tableaux* – that is what I want; and in the background, lying in wait for me, is an ever-increasing longing for the drama. I'm a fool, am I not?[1]

Of course, we all recognize the only possible historical response we can utter to the young Burckhardt's petulant cry. Hardly a 'fool', he wrote in 1860, for example, a book which has long been identified as one of the most important works in nineteenth-century historical studies, *Die Kultur der Renaissance in Italien: Ein Versuch* (translated as *The Civilization of the Renaissance in Italy: An Essay*) (Burckhardt 1958). Even though its particulars are dated and have often been disproved, it is still regarded as the premier model of cultural history. Several commentators, notably Hayden White (1974), Peter Gay (1974), and Karl Weintraub (1966), have called attention to Burckhardt's style or method of composition in this text, the way he writes apart from what he actually says.[2]

I want to pursue that line of enquiry here by investigating how the subject Burckhardt studied – the Italian Renaissance – determined not only the parameters of his historical field in the usual ways, by giving him the materials, texts, peoples, etc., to be investigated, but in some far more mysterious and submerged way also predisposed him to organize its disparate aspects in a way that formally reified the primary visual code of that age. Renaissance art, I will argue, delimited the very configuration in which Burckhardt cast his subject in the first place: the form of the 'tableau' as he referred to it, a scheme of visualization so persuasive that it still may be predetermining the tendency we have today to conceptualize Renaissance Europe as a static figurative and cultural unity.

A gratuitous word here about what cultural history is, or attempts to be, since many historiographers credit Burckhardt with 'inventing' or at least epitomizing, the genre. Burckhardt's protestations to the contrary (as Gombrich, 1969, has shown), cultural history is a commitment to a method of research originally rooted in Hegelian sentiments. The cultural historian *presumes* that there is an interconnectedness (if not, perhaps, a *Zeitgeist per se*) that links the attitudes, artefacts, events, etc., of a certain time and place. Cultural historians are not particularly interested in political events that can be diachronically plotted along the standard time line of historical evolution. Instead their focus is a synchronic or structural one. They arrest time at one specific moment, most likely one particular stylistic period, and trace the gossamer threads through the complex knot they regard as the *cultural* configuration of the age.

Burckhardt was more adept at this manoeuvre, as well as more ambitious, than many of his followers. Little about the Renaissance escaped his purview. The chapters of *The Civilization* treat topics ranging from despotic tyrannies to styles of cosmetics, from neo-Latin poetry to the status of women. Congratulating himself for not making the book three times as thick as it turned out to be,[3] he arrived at an elegantly simple overview of the history of Italy between the fourteenth and sixteenth centuries: it was the period of the 'rediscovery of the world and of man'.

Confident assertions, however, are frequently counter-balanced by his acute sense of the relativity, even the futility, of the historian's enterprise, a rhetorical stance unusual, indeed, for German scholarship in the nineteenth century.[4] In the opening paragraph, he makes it clear why the work is subtitled *Ein Versuch (An Essay)*:

> This work bears the title of an essay in the strictest sense of the word. No one is more conscious than the writer with what limited means and strength he has addressed himself to a task so arduous. . . . *To each eye,* perhaps, the outlines of a given civilization present a different *picture.* . . . In the wide ocean upon which we venture the possible ways

Figure 1. Carpaccio, *Arrival of St Ursula*, 1495. Venice: Accademia.

and directions are many; and the same studies which have served for this work might easily, in other hands, not only receive a wholly different treatment and application, but lead also to essentially different conclusions. (Burckhardt 1958: 21; italics mine)

'Picture' is as revealing a word here as is 'essay'. Having dismissed the necessity for treating this age, as other ages before it had been customarily rendered, by reciting a narrative bound to the chronological inexorability of the events it purports to describe, Burckhardt, the consummate *cicerone*, guides his readers on a richly varied and picturesque tour of the past. What we encounter along the way are scores of forgotten places and hundreds of dusty lives painted once again in the most vivid of colours (as opposed to the noted 'colourlessness' of Ranke), all serving as illustrations of what Gombrich (1969: 18) calls 'the villainies, the gaieties, the feats of prowess, the craving for fame'.

One arbitrarily chosen example will have to serve as a reminder of this pictorially evocative technique (this illustration merely serves to demonstrate the kind of domain from which Burckhardt's narrative emerges, at the same time as it seeks to describe that habitus – there are no one-to-one correspondences here). Compare Carpaccio's painting (Figure 1) to Burckhardt's recounting

> of Venice . . . the jewel-casket of the world . . . where the business of the world is transacted, not amid shouting confusion, but with the subdued hum of many voices; where in the porticos round the square and in those of the adjoining streets sit hundreds of money-changers and goldsmiths, with endless rows of shops and warehouses above their heads. . . . Before . . . the great Fondaco of the Germans . . . ships are drawn up side by side in the canal; higher up is a whole fleet laden with wine and oil, and parallel with it, on the shore swarming with porters, are the vaults of the merchants. (Burckhardt 1958: 83–4)

It is important to recall that the lavish illustrations that decorate this century's editions of *The Civilization* were entirely absent in Burckhardt's original, as were, indeed, even sustained descriptions of works of art.[5] It is solely on the basis of passages such as these (and not because of the illustrations, in other words) that commentators have consistently pointed to Burckhardt's pictorial acuity. The passion for the re-creative aspect of visualization is paramount in his lifelong letters and lectures, as well as in this book. Recall his plaintive yearning for tableaux quoted from his youth. That sentiment was to be reiterated countless times throughout his career, but perhaps never more memorably than in two of his late letters, both addressed to his younger colleague, Friedrich Nietzsche; in the first he extols Nietzsche for his philosophical works by saying that 'my poor head has never been capable of reflecting, even at a distance, as you are able to do, upon final causes, the aims and the desirability of history', and he continues in the second, 'I have never . . . penetrated into the Temple of genuine thought, but have all my life taken delight in the halls and forecourt of the Peribolos, where the image, in the widest sense of the word, reigns.'[6]

The Civilization of the Renaissance is imagistic to be sure; to speak of Burckhardt's work as a 'portrait' has almost become a cliché. Yet the discursive structure by which these images are rendered *visible* has not in itself been a focus of study. The configuration of the essay seems to me to be more revealing of Burckhardt's indebtedness to the mind and material of fifteenth-century Italy than might at first be apparent. I make that claim because of my interest in the generic problem of how an historical period might syntactically 'prefigure' its own historiographic expression, and I think the cultural history of Burckhardt is a good test case for that issue – but more of that in a moment.

The concept of 'prefigurement' is, of course, fundamental to the work of Hayden White; both in his general exploration of the 'tropological' nature of all historical discourse and in his specific analysis of Burckhardt's reliance on certain rhetorical tropes.[7] White's powerful metahistorical achievement has been 'to shift hermeneutic interest from the *content* of texts being investigated to their *formal* properties', in the process 'problematizing' the classic texts of the tradition (White 1982: 282, 289). Historians, he argues, have constructed their manifest historical recitations upon a substructure essentially poetic in nature. This prefigurative level of discourse provides the rules according to which description and argument in the ongoing historical narrative become combined and 'the phases through which the discourse must pass in the process of earning its right of closure'. This 'process of understanding', he claims, 'proceeds by the exploitation of the principal modalities of figuration', the so-called 'master tropes' – in Burckhardt's case, the trope of irony (White 1978: 5).

Burckhardt was beleaguered by an ironic perception of the past. Disenchanted by the failings and inadequacies of the liberal revolutions of his youth, the middle-aged Burckhardt turned increasingly to the philosophy of Schopenhauer for justification of his melancholic observations. He saw the '"culture of *old* Europe" . . . as a ruin' (White 1973: 234), and he despaired that historical events, especially contemporary ones, had any meaning at all. For Schopenhauer, as White has said, genius was evidenced not by 'involvement in the historical process but [by] the capacity to remain a pure spectator' (ibid., 240). The scholarly Burckhardt so put this sentiment into practice that it might well be he whom Nietzsche had in mind when he accused certain historians of regarding themselves as 'mere Epigoni', late-comers whose voyeuristic approach to the past vitiates contemporary moral and political action (Nietzsche 1958: 28–9).[8]

We should take our cue from Nietzsche's remarks. The emphasis on historical *seeing*, as well as historical distance, is crucial. If we are intent on unravelling the signifying structure of Burckhardt's classic text, then the variety of latent codes that come into play in the production of its manifest meanings needs to be addressed. And here is where I would take a route different from, though complementary to, White. To repeat, White has traced Burckhardt's formal indebtedness to a certain timeless rhetorical trope. What I would like to argue is his kindred indebtedness to a particular time-bound

Figure 2. Masaccio, *Adoration of the Magi*, Predella of Pisa Polyptych, 1426. Berlin-Dahlem Museum.

strategy of visual representation. If Burckhardt's visual sense did not prefigure his choice of linguistic strategies, it at least reinforced their selection.

The distinctive kind of cultural history embodied in this text I see as itself dependent upon the quattrocento's own principles of composition, and specifically those articulated in Leon-Battista Alberti's 1435 manuscript, *De Pictura* (Alberti 1972).[9] The virtues of Burckhardt's approach are the virtues of a fifteenth-century illusionistic painting executed in perspective; its problems are akin to those engendered by the act of treating the world perspectivally. This essay is *about* Burckhardt, to be sure, but it is also *about* the tenacity of Renaissance modes of visual re-presentation, since it is through the efforts of that period's painters and theoreticians of art that the nineteenth-century historian has provided the standard model for our thinking: certainly about the thematic unity of the Renaissance, and, perhaps, about the past in general.

Alberti concentrated on two particular aspects of painting: its *istoria* and the deployment of this story according to perspectival principles. For the moment let us consider the first, the *istoria* – the story, the history that is the manifest subject of the painting. The *Adoration of the Magi* (Figure 2) by Masaccio can serve as a case in point.[10] Alberti believed that a painting, in order to edify, i.e. in order to move the soul of the beholder, had to be based on something more than realism. It needed to possess a certain monumentality, a critical element of dramatic content, for painting, he believed, could have the magical power to make 'the absent present . . . and the dead [appear] to the living many centuries later' (Alberti 1972: 61). Even though Masaccio's painting is at least a decade older than his treatise, the treatment of the biblical subject is one of which Alberti would have approved. To create the proper impact, he recommended that the work of art be filled with what he called the 'plentiful variety' of pictorial detail, but not so much that the painting would

Figure 3. Leonardo da Vinci, *Adoration of the Magi*, begun 1481. Florence: Uffizi.

lack dignity. To this end, he claimed that good paintings should include all ages of man – even a few women, and a few animals (ibid., 79). Their trappings should be richly elaborated; their presentation on the canvas carefully controlled through the placement of evocative gestures that clearly indicate the principal story within the extended composition.

It taxes the imagination very little to relate these prescriptions about historical subject-matter to Burckhardt's richly visual narrative. The story he tells is indeed one of larger than life figures, magisterially garbed in antique robes, whose carefully selected words and picturesque actions inevitably gesture towards a greater meaning than they alone possess. All the 'richly varied' and 'abundant' examples of the Renaissance sensibility that Burckhardt collects – from the making of musical instruments to the breaking of marriage customs, essential as each is to the richness of the composition as a whole – *all* are nevertheless employed to a higher end, that goal being the revelation of the spirit of the times.

Yet it is in the control and organization of these complex historical subjects on a formal level, i.e. in assigning 'places' to each, that Burckhardt comes closer still to a Renaissance visual sensibility – in this respect, Leonardo's incomplete interpretation of the same subject of the Adoration is more appropriate (Figure 3). As all art historians know, the content of a work of art is one thing, and the form, the language through which the content is made manifest, is quite another. It is not sufficient (though it is interesting, I think) to point out that Burckhardt composed a vast and formally coherent *istoria*. Instead it is the systematic way in which he accomplished this feat that is significant, and that has to do with Alberti's second prescription, or at least Burckhardt's recognition of that spatial thesis as it was put into practice by successive generations of Renaissance painters.[11] Alberti was not the first, of course, to discover the laws of perspective, but he was the first to codify them, to set out their application as they pertain to the arrangement of space on the artist's canvas (see Edgerton, 1975).

Briefly put, the geometricization of space that Alberti codified involves a system for converting three-dimensional 'reality' to two-dimensional space. To this end, he laid out a grid of converging lines whose rationale lies with the viewer outside the picture plane (Figures 4 and 5). A painting such as the 1504 *Betrothal* by Raphael (Burckhardt's favourite Renaissance painter) is put together according to very precise mathematical principles (e.g. since we assume that all the tiles in the piazza are the same size, we read their progressive diminution as a recession into space). Late-fifteenth-century painters manipulated this geometricizing and abstracting scheme with increasing virtuosity, and Burckhardt was an admiring connoisseur of their efforts. But there is more implied in the adoption of a perspectival scheme than the mastery of certain mathematical effects. Once obeyed, these rules serve what Alberti saw as the higher significance of the painting, again the *istoria*. All appears in proportion, nothing seems out of place, each of the parts fits nobly together, one to the other.

Especially noteworthy for my analysis of Burckhardt's point of view is the fact that the organon through which the visual field is systematized, this Albertian graph of space, is dependent upon somebody outside looking in, an external viewer whose directed gaze singularly justifies the arrangement and placement of the rich and copious details of the optical field. Long after the first fifteenth-century dogmatic devotion to translating this geometric system into paint had waned, sixteenth-century painters continued to appropriate its

Figure 4. Raphael, *Betrothal of the Virgin*, 1504. Pinacoteca di Brera.

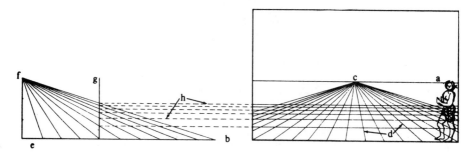

Figure 5. Design of Alberti's perspective construction. *a*, height of human being, *b*, base line, *c*, vanishing point, *d*, orthogonals, *e*, 'little space', *f*. distance point, *g*, vertical intersection, *h*, transversals. Reprinted from F. Hartt, *History of Italian Renaissance Art* (Prentice Hall).

thematic implications. A Renaissance painting 'is a construct and the viewer exists in a temporal sense "before" the represented world' (Białostocki 1985: 523).[12] A perspective painting is a lesson in the logic of representation (see Bryson 1983: 106).

Whom did it teach? What does all this have to do with Burckhardt? Above all, consider his position as an historian. He often referred to his perspective on the past as one originating from an Archimedean point of view.[13] In his letters, he is always the melancholic observer on the other side of history, the outsider looking in, the spectator who admires but can never inhabit the sunny vistas from which he is separated in time. From the greyness of the industrial north, he writes: 'I . . . at least want to discover the interest for which I am to perish . . . namely, the old culture of Europe.'[14] The world-weary tone of his lamentations highlights both his sense of severance from the past, and his languorous desire to re-create it. 'This', he exclaimed, 'is where I stand on the shore of the world – stretching out my arms towards the *fons et origo* of all things, and that is why history to me is sheer poetry.'[15]

Like Alberti's distanced artist/observer, Burckhardt the historian could begin the world anew, or at least create compositions whose formal consistency is solely dependent upon his single perspective. 'To each eye,' he said in the introduction, 'the outlines of a given civilization present a different picture.' The eyes of most historians, however, had been glazed over by political recitations. For Burckhardt, who sees history as a poetic activity, no such dimness is possible. He envisions the Renaissance as a vast tableau, in which, according to Karl Weintraub, 'the confusing multiplicity of details becomes a unified construct, having internal structure, coherence and meaning' (Weintraub 1966: 5). 'The shape of Burckhardt's *Kultur der Renaissance*', asserts Peter Gay, 'was an aesthetic choice designed to make a substantive point: the Renaissance was, in Burckhardt's view, a coherent entity pervaded by a common spirit' (Gay 1974: 171).

All good *istoriae* are harmonically ordered according to the 'imperious'[16] perspectives of their creators, not necessarily according to the dictates of their own intrinsic order. Formal coherence is itself the supreme virtue of the historian's exposition, as it is the glory of the Renaissance artist. The story of politics should not dominate the story of art; the birth of a new self-consciousness should not overshadow the dependence on Christian dogma. The constant balancing of equivalents is the key, for only through such an act of distant viewing will the typical emerge from the out-of-the-ordinary, the spirit of the age arise from the ashes of its details.[17]

Each aspect of the age, from the book-learning of the princes to the medicinal probings of the doctors, fits together as neatly as the tiles in Raphael's piazza. And what is more, all achieve this appearance of regularity and harmony because they derive their legitimacy from the historian who directs their arrangement from without. As any late-fifteenth-century cartographer knew, one cannot easily draw a map when standing within the territory. In 1860, the Renaissance was still *uncharted*, and it was Burckhardt himself who first gave ideological shape and significance to its study: he once said he would like to see 'the mosaic of peoples and civilizations' conceived of as a 'vast . . . map . . . embracing both the material and spiritual worlds' (Burckhardt 1948: 83–4; see also Gay 1974: 149).

What I am suggesting is that Burckhardt learned from the painters 'how to look, to visualize': an important lesson since he at all times avowed that 'our historical pictures are . . . pure constructions'.[18] Historical knowledge is an act of 'pure seeing' (White 1973: 233). The Renaissance technique of perspectival picturing was particularly germane to the structural purposes of Burckhardt's kind of history writing, for cultural history depends ultimately on the premiss that the world of the past can be gathered together 'as an external image'.[19] Pieces fall into place; parts become wholes. And the final meaning of the *istoria* transcends any one of its individual aspects, although that meaning is inevitably dependent on the viewpoint of him or her who orders it.

An historical text is like an historical painting executed in perspective. Certain subjects and figures should be highlighted; others should more properly retreat into the shadows. Beauty of form is what matters (especially if one was presenting this picture as an antidote to the squalor of the nineteenth century with its 'great wheeled machines' as he called them).[20] Like Raphael, Burckhardt strove for harmony and balance in his compositions. He praised Raphael as a history painter for his organic balancing of equivalents. No one theme excludes the others; no detail pushes forward to intrude upon the whole. As an example, here is his earlier description from the *Cicerone* of the *School of Athens* (Figure 6):

> the wonderfully beautiful hall, which forms the background, [is] not merely a picturesque idea, but a consciously intended symbol of the healthy harmony between the powers of the soul and the mind. In such a building one could not but feel happy. Raphael has translated the whole thought and learning of antiquity entirely into lively demonstration and earnest listening . . . . We find in the picture a most excellent arrangement of the teachers, listeners, and spectators, easy movement in the space, richness without crowding, complete harmony of the picturesque and dramatic motives. (Burckhardt 1908: 151).[21]

Raphael's spatial arrangements are the mark of his genius. He is the 'great historical painter, who can distinguish the characteristic from the accidental, the permanent from the transitory' (ibid., 139) and like Goethe, he possesses the wisdom of *Anschauung*, the visual ability to 'grasp, through observation aided by intuition, a thing in its wholeness' (Heller 1957: 74).

In many ways, these are the very tasks that Burckhardt intentionally set before himself as an historian. Dealing as he must with such a wide array of customs, beliefs, institutions, artefacts, and personalities of the age, he too had to grasp the essential harmonic order that would lend meaning and coherence to the whole, that would elicit the spirit of the age out of its thousand and one expressions, that would 'distinguish the characteristic from the accidental'. The way he mastered this challenge, a challenge which the scope of his cultural history of necessity imposed upon him, seems to me to be indebted directly to the infrastructure, the 'stylistic architecture' (Gay 1974: 171) of the paintings that were already providing him with vivid examples of subject-matter.

It should be stressed that the geometricizing qualities of Albertian perspective were not the aspects that I am claiming Burckhardt conspicuously appropriated. If they were, to be literal about it, we would have to identify a vanishing point, the exact posing of symmetries, a horizon line, proportional diminution, a gesturing figure divided into thirds, etc. Although it could be carried out to a degree, such an exercise in literal reductionism would verge on the ridiculous.

Figure 6. Raphael, *School of Athens*, 1510–11. Vatican.

Instead, it is the synthesizing end to which these principles were intuitively put by subsequent Renaissance painters whom he admired (many, indeed, violated the rigidity of Alberti's graph) that Burckhardt emulated in his own perspectivalism: the creation of an ordered harmonious *istoria*, temporally and spatially framed, and one dependent upon a singularly creative and sympathetic eye. These mandates may not be literally perspectival (i.e. mathematical), but they certainly are metaphorically so (as they were in the art of Raphael).

Granted, Renaissance art appealed to Burckhardt for many reasons, but not the least of which was its ability to deify the viewer in some way, by making the world of the painting dependent upon his or her monocular viewpoint. Everything exists in a formal relationship to the observer. With his strange, melancholic disposition, Burckhardt was well suited to appreciate the power of such a vantage point. Yet such a recognition could have been as much a source of anxiety as it was a source of security. Burckhardt knew that no one point of view was ever sufficient for overcoming the predicament of onesidedness, and that is undoubtedly why he so often emphasized the tenuousness of his conclusions.

Of course, no reader of Burckhardt can help but notice how far removed in sentiment this nineteenth-century ideology of perspective is from that of the fifteenth century. In the Renaissance, it was conceived to be an empowering mode, a mathematical development linked to astronomy, cartography, even the evolution of a patently scientific point of view. In the nineteenth century, by contrast, Nietzsche could openly mock the naïveté of claims to objectivity by satirizing them: 'as though there would be a world left over once we subtracted the perspectival'.[22] The formal modality of one century has been filled with very different significance by the temperament of another.

The form of a narrative, as many semioticians have pointed out, is where a text 'does its ideologically significant work' (White 1982: 300). It follows that Burckhardt's adoption of the idea of history as pure seeing from a remote perspective has political implications. Born in the same year (1818) as Marx, Burckhardt hardly shared his revolutionary understanding of the course of history. Although he flirted with liberal causes as a youth in the turbulent atmosphere of the early 1840s, by the middle of the decade the young scholar claimed to be historically outside the ideological fracas. In 1846 he wrote to a friend who was a nationalist sympathizer:

None of you has any idea yet what a people is and how easily it deteriorates into a barbarous mob. You do not know yet what a tyrannical rule is to be set up over the spirit. . . . We may all perish; but I for one shall choose the cause for which I am going to perish: the culture of old Europe.[23]

His desire to 'emancipate' himself from the inexorability of time and change and to 'seek reward in the sublimity of a self-detached vision', as Heller (1957: 87) puts it, gave him the assurance that to 'act' was meaningless. Such perspectivalism also had profound historiographic consequences. 'There is a good deal of violence in Burckhardt's *Kultur der Renaissance*,' says Peter Gay, 'much strain and tension, but they are all subsumed under the grand *composition* of his vast, crowded, but harmonious *canvas*' (Gay 1974: 171; italics mine). He even turned his analysis of sanguinary Florentine politics into a seminal chapter entitled 'The state as a work of art'.

The politically charged aspects of the Renaissance were compartmentalized and domesticated as they assumed their static position alongside its more culturally creative manifestations.[24] 'The background is for me the main thing, and the background is the subject of cultural history, to which I mainly want to devote myself,' he wrote to a friend in 1842 (Gilbert 1986: 249). Having dispersed the elements of the age against this grid or backdrop of compositional coherence, thereby preordaining the kinds of relationships that exist among them, his cultural configuration was complete. It had little connection with matters outside its spatial and temporal frame except to be a point of reference against which Burckhardt could descry his own century's cultural degeneration. This point of view, once adopted, mandates that the historian be a passive (though creative) chronicler, not a political activist. For Burckhardt, as White says, 'the truths taught by history were melancholy ones. They led neither to hope nor to action. They did not even suggest that humanity itself would *endure*' (White 1973: 230).

Even though I have been speaking directly about the origin of Burckhardt's history writing, I am interested in the larger issue of what sometimes seems to be a hermeneutic overlap between the materials of an historical age and its historiographic expression. Could it be that the structure of a period's consciousness determines not just the array of things that can be said about it, but also, at times, formally legislates *how* these things are said? Could not the perspective system initiated by Alberti, in other words, be construed not only as a painterly mechanism for locating objects spatially in relation to one another, but also as an enduring cognitive schema that provided a narrative architectonic for the cultural historian who desired to relate objects and people and attitudes temporally? I have here been arguing that Renaissance paintings presented Burckhardt with a strategy for representing the Renaissance.

The principal criterion for historical knowledge usually implies a difference between the perceiving apparatus and the structure under observation. What is slightly disconcerting about pointing out Burckhardt's indebtedness to Renaissance principles of composition is that this argument could suggest that a large body of historiography – the cultural history of the Renaissance, and perhaps even the notion of cultural history in general – might well be a function of the system that it is purporting to describe and define. Burckhardt's history is a part of what it is looking at. Instead of being an analytic of the period, it is an analogue of a Renaissance procedure. Subject and object interpenetrate.

Like the painter of a canvas perspectivally gridded, the cultural historian approaches her or his subject with the confidence that she or he will discover an order into which all the disparate and colourful parts of the story can fit. True enough, this order may be dependent upon her or his point of view, as Burckhardt believed, but again as in a painting executed in perspective, the position of the artist must be fixed in relation to the pictorial field. The artist/historian becomes the absent observer of the action. Her or his vantage point having been established, things tend to fall into place around this anchor of perception.[25]

The historical subject once ordered (even if subjectively) assumes all the characteristics of an exercise in objectivity. If it works, it does not appear possible for matters to be other than they are. As Theodore Mommsen predicted, Burckhardt's words would still ring true, 'though every sentence in them should stand in need of correction by advancing research'.[26] The relationship between an objective point of view and the 'discovery' of a hidden order is a curious one, however. An objective viewpoint should be established inductively, but as several recent philosophers of science keep telling us, no such procedure is really ever possible. Everything takes place within a paradigmatic framework, so that all investigations of any sort conform to a predetermined formal harmony.

The paradigmatic framework within which Jacob Burckhardt proceeded, I have been arguing, is one that is at least partially indebted to the mandates of perspectival picturing. His history is as persuasive, as artful, as an early Renaissance painting. Indeed. But it is also a composition that ensnares us in its problematic vision.

The paradigm of perspective is one fraught with stunning ambiguities, for as employed in the history and philosophy of art, it is used both as an example of objectivity and as an example of the mythology of objectivity. It is a tenet of art history that styles change, but perspective remains, curiously, always the constant standard against which to judge various artistic movements and their representational agenda. Perspective, apart from its origins, is frequently treated as something 'scientific' – something outside time. It is not just another 'mapping method', Gombrich (1972: 138) has claimed. If we want to transcribe our spatial experience of the three-dimensional world on to a two-dimensional canvas, then the laws of perspective show us how to do it. It is not just a visual trick. Its legitimacy is corroborated by photography, proved by perceptual psychologists.

If we were to array on two sides the list of names of those who believe perspective is Accurate, and those who consider it a Convention, statistically the former would win. But perhaps this common stock of assertions is just another example, in a long line of examples, of the cultural imperialism of this form of representation. Marx Wartofsky has argued that the perspective of the Renaissance has become the 'perspective of the world' (Wartofsky 1980: 140). This particular pictorial convention still holds us in its grip. It has taught us how to see. So we, perhaps, do not exactly *see* it for what it is.

Those who testify to the conventionality of linear perspective do not argue whether or not the system works according to optical laws and the laws of geometry – it does. The more problematic question is why do we think the laws of geometry 'accurately' transcribe what we see? This is the issue: how it is a convention and not a convention at the same time. James Ackerman has said, if you want 'to communicate as precise a record of fact' as you can, 'follow Alberti'. If you wish to communicate how things look, follow no one.[27]

The system of perspective is not just a form of representation, a representational device, but a representational device that also possesses a thematic content. It is a part, or a symptom, or a cause, of a particular, to use Baxandall's term, 'visual culture'.[28] It affects other cultural products as much as it is affected by them. This is what Panofsky (1924–5) meant by calling perspective 'a symbolic form'. It is not just the physics of the eye, but the metaphysics of Renaissance culture that perspective exemplifies, for it is an expression of a desire to order the world in a certain way: to make incoherencies coherent, to objectify subjective points of view, to turn the shimmering world of visual experience into a richly fixated construct.

Because his historiographic aims are similar, I have been interpreting the role of perspective as a symbolic form in the work of Burckhardt as well. The constant study of Renaissance paintings cultivated his viewing sense, I am claiming, in more than an indirect way. The rationalization of sight perfected in the fifteenth century has ever since implied 'the notion that reality itself is pictorial' (Heelan 1983: 102). Regardless of whether or not we see perspectivally, this system of sight has been adopted for much more than optical verisimilitude. In the Renaissance world, one might contend, it was used for backgrounding, foregrounding, hierarchizing, the justifying of social relationships in general.[29] Perhaps it is itself, in part, the originator of the modern interest in coherence – of writing history, say, as the discovery of the hidden order of things. The very idea that a scholarly project has to produce an ordered vision from afar is especially apparent in Burckhardt. As his chapter headings make clear, the cultural historian discovers symmetries and relationships behind the chaos of appearances. Perspective provides a means of fixing the world (historical or otherwise) against the mutability of life. It functions as a kind of grid or map that can be applied at will.

It is interesting, in this respect, to contrast Burckhardt's perspectival thinking with that of Michel Foucault, whose work, at least in relation to other works of cultural history, is anti-perspectival. Foucault seems deliber-

Figure 7. Fra Angelico, *St Lawrence Distributing Alms*, 1447–50. Vatican.

ately to adopt an eccentric point of view in order to be able to extract deeds and ideas from their perspective context and magnify or diminish them extraordinarily. So too do the works of many *Annales* scholars. The history of cod fishing, for example, is lifted out of its typically minuscule part in the narrative context of early modern Europe and magnified in importance beyond all expectations. The inevitable result of such a project – so identifiable as a twentieth-century work of art – is an explosion of perspectival hegemony.[30]

To return to Burckhardt. I think it is intriguing to contemplate why many historians, not to say most thinkers in general, are driven to think perspectivally, to creating worlds where all things fall into place. In this sense – and contrary to the Renaissance interpretation of the system – perspective is not liberating. It is dogmatic and doctrinaire. It admits no disjunctions or contrarieties into its scheme. By contrast, the medieval treatment of space could be construed as creatively freeing.

As examples, consider these two portraits of the popular St Lawrence, one by Fra Angelico, the other a manuscript page from the late medieval *Hours* of Catherine of Cleves (Figures 7 and 8). The space of the Renaissance painting is delimited by, or perhaps can never even escape, the perspectival gaze of the viewer. The regimentation of the scheme is convincingly continued into the distance and seems to promise an order without end. The architectural motifs, beautifully framing the central scene, St Lawrence dispensing the treasures of the Church, become an elaboration of that control. The medieval book of hours, on the other hand, presents a completely different conception of space as well as subject. The fish that engagingly intertwine in the 'non-space' of the margins certainly rival in both their detail and scale the tiny saint whose martyrdom merits the doubly framed position in the middle of the page. The medieval artist never seems to have considered the possibility of constructing one uniform space, let alone one subject. The cornucopia of existence pours objects on to the page with choreographed abandon.

The Middle Ages, for Burckhardt, had been an age (in his words) of 'all foreground(s) . . . without perspective'. 'By the year 1200, at the height of the Middle Ages', he wrote,

a genuine, hearty enjoyment of the external world was again in existence, and found lively expression in the minstrelsy of different nations, which gives evidence of the sympathy felt with all the simple phenomena of nature – spring with its flowers, the green fields, and the woods [Figure 9]. . . . [But] from these poems, it would never be guessed that their noble authors in all countries inhabited or visited lofty castles commanding distant prospects. (Burckhardt 1958: 293)

Like a Renaissance artist (Figure 10) or humanist, Burckhardt yearned for the commanding vantage point. Consider, in this respect, his poignant recounting of Petrarch's ascent of Mt Ventoux:

> The ascent of a mountain for its own sake was unheard of, and there could be no thought of the companionship of friends or acquaintances. . . . [He] struggled forward and upward, till the clouds lay beneath [his] feet, and at last [he] reached the top. . . . His whole past life, with all its follies, rose before his mind; he remembered that ten years ago that day he had quitted Bologna a young man, and turned a longing gaze toward his native country; he opened a book which was then his constant companion, the *Confessions of St Augustine*, and his eye fell on the passage in the tenth chapter, 'and men go forth, and admire lofty mountains and broad seas, and roaring torrents, and the ocean, and the course of the stars, and forget their own selves while doing so'. (Burckhardt 1958: 296).

Was it Burckhardt, perhaps, whom Nietzsche had more sympathetically in mind when he spoke of history's 'real value' as being located 'in raising the popular melody to a universal symbol and showing what a world of depth, power and beauty exists in it'? For the younger philosopher says (in a passage suggestively reminiscent of that of Burckhardt just quoted) that such an understanding

> requires above all a great artistic faculty, a creative vision from a height, the loving study of the data of experience. . . . We think of the aesthetic phenomenon of the detachment from all personal concern with which the painter sees the picture and forgets himself, in a stormy landscape, amid thunder and lightning, or on a rough sea; and we require the same artistic vision and absorption in his object from the historian. (Nietzsche 1874: 39, 37).[31]

Burckhardt too was possessed of an 'indefinable longing for a distant panorama', and like Dante or Leonardo, as his passage shows, he could evoke by 'a few vigorous lines the sense of the morning airs and the trembling light on the distant ocean, or . . . the grandeur of the storm-beaten forest' (ibid.: 296, 294). If it is not stretching the poetic parallel too far (but we are in pursuit of the genesis of his historical poetics), I would also suggest that Burckhardt, like Petrarch, contemplated his vision through the text of another, a spiritual guide of an age long past. As Petrarch could only appreciate the expansive vision before him in terms of the words of St Augustine, so Burckhardt was instructed by the Renaissance logic of representation. 'The true discoverer', he once said,

> is not the man who first chances to stumble upon anything, but the man who finds what he has sought. Such a one alone stands in a link with the

Figure 8. Master of Catherine of Cleves, *St Lawrence*, c. 1440–45 Ms 91. Pierpont-Morgan Library.

Figure 9. *The Hunt of the Unicorn*, Unicorn Tapestries, *c.* 1500. Cloisters.

thoughts and interests of his predecessors, and this relationship will also determine the account he gives of his search. (ibid.: 280).

The geography of Renaissance painting taught Burckhardt, in part, how to map the Renaissance world. Throughout the two volumes of this panoramic survey of Italian cultural history, Burckhardt's organization, his deployment of information, his hierarchy of subject-matters, his foregrounding and backgrounding of issues, can be seen as produced by a principle akin to Albertian perspective which itself contributed to the production of the Renaissance. Interest in the past is, of course, often provoked by an encounter with the visual artefacts it has left behind (see Potts 1985) and this was avowedly the case with Burckhardt. What we do not always suspect is how

Figure 10. Leonardo da Vinci, *Storm over Valley*, c. 1500. Windsor: Royal Library.

the representation of the past in the historical account might itself be indebted to the representational standards under scrutiny.

Some ages seem to have a way of perpetuating their own formative principles in historical narratives.[32] There is a kind of relationship established between the secondary order of discourse and the original order of things that bridges the gap of time which separates the historian from the period and makes the historical reconstruction at least formally congruent with the age it describes. The historical narrative then becomes an icon of the essential structural unity of the time it is attempting to ensnare. Burckhardt's history, in other words, not only depicted the Renaissance, but also in a sense was itself depicted by the Renaissance. Through Burckhardt, one could argue, Alberti's perspective has made the Renaissance visible to us.

University of Rochester, New York

NOTES

Research for this article has been supported by a National Endowment for the Humanities Fellowship. In a variety of earlier versions, it was presented at the University of Virginia, Yale University, the University of St Andrews, and, finally, at a symposium on the History of the Human Sciences at the University of Durham in the fall of 1986.

1 Letter of 10 June 1844, in Burckhardt (1955).
2 See also Stephen Bann (1981, 1984).
3 Letter of 1 August 1860, in Burckhardt (1955).
4 It should be pointed out that Ranke's famed political histories were not simply exercises in empiricism, although his successors in this tradition present another story. One of his principal concerns was to make the writing of history an evocative, mimetic project. See the preface to Ranke (1874; first published 1824).
5 The first illustrations to *The Civilization* appeared in the fifteenth edition published in Leipzig in 1926, with illustrations collected by Dr Johannes Jahn, an assistant in the Art Historical Institute at the University of Leipzig (published in English in 1929 to accompany the new edition of S. G. C. Middlemore's 1878 translation). Part of the explanation for the lack of illustrations in the original lies in the fact that Burckhardt intended to add a pendant volume treating art history exclusively, with the first work (this one) serving as a kind of preface to this culminating opus (only a fragment was ever published: 'Geschichte der Renaissance in Italien', in F. Kugler (1867); see also *The Architecture of the Italian Renaissance*, trans. J. Palmer and ed. P. Murray, London: 1985). Yet he also undeniably viewed art as something unique, something distinct from other cultural products, and he remained curiously formalistic in his accounts of this supreme cultural achievement. His *Cicerone* of 1855 (Burckhardt 1908) became the model for all his subsequent art historical scholarship. Literature, politics, science, philosophy – each, he granted, was rooted in a specific context. Yet art stands alone; art is self-referential. And it was, paradoxically, the cultural historian Burckhardt who first encouraged his student Wölfflin to develop a 'living law of forms' which would sever the discussion of art from the discussion of milieu, subject-matter, artistic biography, etc. (letter of 2 August 1879, in Burckhardt 1955; see his correspondence with Wölfflin in Gantner 1948).

6 Letters of 5 February 1874 and 5 April 1879, in Burckhardt (1955).

7 In addition to *Metahistory* (White 1973), see *Tropics of Discourse: Essays in Cultural Criticism* (White 1978).

8 For the relationship between Burckhardt and Nietzsche, see Martin (1945), and 'Burckhardt and Nietzsche' in Heller (1957).

9 The complete works of Alberti were published in five volumes in Florence from 1843 to 1849.

10 Svetlana Alpers suggested the example of the predella of Masaccio's Pisa polyptych.

11 Baxandall (1971) emphasizes that Alberti would never have approved of the pursuit of *copia* at the expense of *compositio*; '*copia* must be subordinated to *compositio*'. Paul Barolsky reminds me of the origin of these concepts in the categories of Renaissance rhetorical practice.

12 For a fuller discussion of the cultural hegemony of Italian Renaissance art theory, see Alpers (1983).

13 For example, see Burckhardt 1955: 5 and Burckhardt 1948.

14 Letter of 5 May 1846, in Burckhardt (1955).

15 Letter of 19 June 1842, in Burckhardt (1955).

16 Gay (1974: 171) is using the word in a somewhat different context.

17 See Weintraub's discussion (1966: 131–7) of Burckhardt's use of *Aequivalente*.

18 See Weintraub (1966: 13); also cited in White (1973: 251).

19 Cited in Weintraub (1966: 137).

20 Letter of 17 October 1855, in Burckhardt (1955).

21 From *Cicerone: Eine Anleitung zum Genuss der Kunstwerke Italiens*; published in 1855. Translated as *An Art Guide to Painting in Italy*, by A. Clough in 1908.

22 Nietzsche (1958: 705). I thank Alisdair MacIntyre for this reference. I realize, of course, that Burckhardt and Nietzsche are employing the concept of perspectivalism in slightly different ways.

23 Letter of 5 March 1846, in Burckhardt (1955). Cited in Heller (1957: 81). Compare a similarly morbid sentiment expressed in a letter of a week earlier: 'You weather-wise fellows vie with each other in getting deeper and deeper into this wretched age – I on the other hand have secretly fallen out with it entirely, and for that reason am escaping from it to the beautiful, lazy south, where history is dead, and I, who am so tired of the present, will be refreshed by the thrill of antiquity as by some wonderful and peaceful tomb. Yes, I want to get away from them all, from the radicals, the communists, the industrialists, the intellectuals, the pretentious, the reasoners, the abstract, the absolute, the philosophers, the sophists, the State fanatics, the idealists, the "ists" and "isms" of every kind' (letter of 28 February 1846, in Burckhardt 1955).

24 A frequent criticism of Burckhardt's cultural history is that it ignores the processes of dynamic change in history. See Burke (1986).

25 See Bryson 1983: 106: 'the vanishing point is the anchor of a system which *incarnates* the viewer, renders him tangible and corporeal, a measurable, and above all a visible object in a world of absolute visibility'.

26 Quoted in the introduction to Burckhardt (1970: 54).

27 James Ackerman, cited in Alpers (1983: 45).

28 Michael Baxandall, cited in Alpers (1983: xxv). See Baxandall (1985).

29 It is interesting to compare Macaulay's historical project: 'History has its foreground and its background; and it is principally in the management of its perspective that one artist differs from another. Some events must be represented on a large scale, others diminished; the great majority will be lost in the dimness of the horizon; and a general idea of their joint effect will be given by a few slight touches.' From his 1828 essay on 'History', cited in Bann (1984: 29).

30 I am indebted to an unpublished paper by Grant Holly for this idea.

31 But he is not entirely sympathetic: 'it is only a superstition to say that the picture given to such a man by the object really shows the truth of things. Unless it be that objects are expected in such moments to paint or photograph themselves by their own activity on a purely passive medium!' (Nietzsche 1874: 37).

32 Cultural historians who begin their study of a period by way of its works of art seem most prone to this process of cultural fabrication. Henry Adams's recitation of the cultural context of Mont-St-Michel and Chartres is another apt example.

BIBLIOGRAPHY

Alberti, L. B. (1972) *On Painting*, trans. Cecil Grayson, from *De Pictura* (1435), London: Phaidon Press.

Alpers, S. (1983) *The Art of Describing: Dutch Art in the Seventeenth Century*, Chicago: University of Chicago Press.

Bann, S. (1981) 'Towards a critical historiography: recent work in the philosophy of history', *Philosophy* 56: 365–85.

Bann, S. (1984) *The Clothing of Clio: A Study of the Representation of History in Nineteenth-Century Britain and France*, Cambridge: Cambridge University Press.

Baxandall, M. (1971) *Giotto and the Orators: Humanist Observers of Painting in Italy and the Discovery of Pictorial Composition, 1350–1450*, Oxford: Oxford University Press.

Baxandall, M. (1985) *Patterns of Intention: On the Historical Explanation of Pictures*, New Haven Conn.: Yale University Press.

Białostocki, J. (1985) 'Review of Alpers' *Art of Describing*', *Art Bulletin* 67: 520–6.

Bryson, N. (1983) *Vision and Painting: The Logic of the Gaze*, New Haven, Conn.: Yale University Press.

Burckhardt, J. (1908) *An Art Guide to Painting in Italy*, trans. A. H. Clough, London: T. Werner Laurie.

Burckhardt, J. (1948) *Force and Freedom*, ed. J. H. Nichols, New York: Pantheon Books.

Burckhardt, J. (1955) *The Letters of Jacob Burckhardt*, ed. and trans. Alexander Dru, New York: Pantheon Books.

Burckhardt, J. (1958) *The Civilization of the Renaissance in Italy*, 2 volumes, ed. B. Nelson and C. Trinkaus, New York: Harper & Row.

Burckhardt, J. (1985) *The Architecture of the Italian Renaissance*, trans. by J. Palmer, rev. and ed. by P. Murray, London: University of Chicago Press.

Burke, P. (1986) 'Cultural history: past, present and future', *Theoretische Geschiedenis* 13: 187–96.

Edgerton, S. (1975) *The Renaissance Rediscovery of Linear Perspective*, New York: Harper & Row.

Gantner, J. (ed.) (1948) *Jacob Burckhardt and Heinrich Wöfflin: Briefwechsel und andere Dokumente ihrer Begegnung, 1882–1897*, Basel: B. Schwabe.

Gay, P. (1974) *Style in History*, New York: McGraw-Hill.

Gilbert, F. (1986) 'Jacob Burckhardt's student years: the road to cultural history', *Journal of the History of Ideas* 47: 249–74.

Gombrich, E. (1969) *In Search of Cultural History*, Oxford: Oxford University Press.

Gombrich, E. (1972) 'The "what" and the "how": perspective, representation and the phenomenal world', in R. Rudner and I. Scheffler (eds), *Logic and Art: Essays in Honor of Nelson Goodman*, Indianapolis: Bobbs-Merrill.

Heelan, P. (1983) *Space-Perception and the Philosophy of Science*, Berkeley, Calif.: University of California Press.

Heller, E. (1957) *The Disinherited Mind: Essays in Modern German Literature and Thought*, Cleveland, Ohio: Meridian Books.

Kugler, F. (1867) *Geschichte der Baukunst*, Stuttgart: Ebner & Seubert.

Martin, A. (1945) *Nietzsche und Burckhardt: Zwei Geistige Welten im Dialog*, Basel: Ernst Reinhardt.

Nietzsche, F. (1874) *The Use and Abuse of History*, trans. A. Collins, Indianapolis, Ind.: Bobbs-Merrill.

Nietzsche, F. (1958) *Aus dem Nachlass der Achtzigerjahre*, ed. K. Schlechta, Munich: Hanser.

Panofsky, E. (1924–5) 'Die Perspektive als "symbolische Form"', *Vorträge der Bibliothek Warburg*, Leipzig/Berlin, 7.

Potts, A. (1985) 'What is the history of art?', *History Today* 35: 37–8.

Ranke, L. von (1874) *Geschichten der romanischen und germanischen Volker von 1494 bis 1514*, 2 volumes, 2nd edn, Leipzig: Duncker und Humblot.

Wartofsky, M. (1980) 'Visual scenarios: the role of representation in visual perception', in M. A. Hagen (ed.), *The Perception of Pictures*, New York: Academic Press.

Weintraub, K. (1966) *Visions of Culture*, Chicago: University of Chicago Press.

White, H. (1974) *Metahistory: The Historical Imagination in Nineteenth-Century Europe*, Baltimore, NJ: Johns Hopkins University Press.

White, H. (1978) *Tropics of Discourse: Essays in Cultural Criticism*, Baltimore, NJ: Johns Hopkins University Press.

White, H. (1982) 'Method and ideology in intellectual history: the case of Henry Adams', in D. LaCapra and S. Kaplan (eds), *Modern European Intellectual History: Reappraisals and New Perspectives*, Ithaca: Cornell University Press.

Representing the real: Gros' paintings of Napoleon

NORMAN BRYSON

I

I want here to examine two paintings by Gros – *The Plague-House at Jaffa* (Fig. 1) and *The Battlefield of Eylau* (Fig. 2) – and to make the claim that they are, realistic. Since both works are full of the kind of observed-looking detail and seemingly transcriptive registration with which Gros famously departed from Davidian precedent, the claim that these paintings are realistic might seem too flat to be worth making. But the kind of realism I have in mind, and which these two works I think embody, is not at all the realism that might be alleged to come from high fidelity transcription of the real world, or even from the 'effect of the real' as Barthes described it.

It is true that these works of Gros strike one as realistic in quite obvious ways. For one thing, Gros' colour range has freed itself from the static Davidian chords, notably the triad scarlet-tan-blue. Where David's repetition of certain privileged colours serves to guarantee that his history paintings are *not* in the orbit of anecdotal realism, Gros' suspension of that restriction upon colour choice seems, conversely, to guarantee that his paintings have in them an on-the-spot faithfulness to appearance. Knowing that Gros' extended colour range owes however much to Rubens or to other sources need not lessen the force of this guarantee: Rubens can easily be thought to supply Gros with the colour means that enabled him to make his minute colour adjustments on the spot, to supply Gros with schemata much better at scanning the colours of the real world than those supplied by David.

Gros seems equally liberated from David's restrictions on posture. Where in David one senses that key poses are chosen because, among the many poses available in the tradition, these are the ones which most suggest statuary, which show the body *passing through* sculpture, in Gros one senses kinetic forces David never deals with. Gros' postures are selected for quite other

Figure 1. Gros, *The Plague-House at Jaffa*. Paris: Louvre.

reasons: the body is thought of as moving on a scale between extremes of energy and of lassitude: the energetic end expressed in forms too fleeting to be thought of as sculptural in David's sense; and the drained or motionless end equated simply with death. Gros' postures refer to a scale of vital energy, so much so that where he does use Davidian formulae – for instance, the Davidian grid which forces arms to move parallel to the picture plane, and heads to move into full profile or full frontal positions – he seems to be regressing to an academic manner which does not square with his other aims as a painter.

One could multiply such instances of obvious realism in Gros, and it would be interesting if one's observations altogether escaped one of the dominant ways of thinking about this painter: as a realist struggling against the moribund but compelling formulae of neo-classicism. When this struggle is described in Bloomian terms, as the agon of Gros against David, I think the account extraordinarily sensitive to the recorded facts of Gros' output as a whole, but the elaboration I have in mind is not in terms of Bloom but rather of common sense.[1] This tells us that Gros found that the schemata received from David had to be revised drastically in order to depict the visual reality of places as exotic as Jaffa and Eylau. The Davidian formulae were matched

Figure 2. Gros, *The Battlefield of Eylau*. Paris: Louvre.

against the field and found wanting; colour-schemata from Rubens and compositional formulae from baroque quickly replaced the Davidian legacy, though bits are retained, and sometimes we see throwbacks, such as the flattened frieze-space around Napoleon and his generals in *Eylau*, or the similarly flattened space, and profiles and full frontal heads, in *Jaffa*.

This account provides at least a coherent way of talking about Gros' style, yet its common-sense version of what realism might be drowns out another description of Gros as a realist which I think is rather more interesting. It is also rather elusive. In order to reach that other kind of realism I will first have to draw some distinctions between different uses of the word 'real'; and then trace a brief history of the kind of realism I have in mind, as it passes on to Gros from David.

II

Discussions of realism, especially in current literary criticism, often begin by invoking a simple *reflection* version of realism, which is then ousted by a more sophisticated account, sometimes of a semiological nature. I am afraid the present discussion is no exception. In a number of influential accounts of visual representation, the image is said simply to reduplicate a prior world. In order to create the representation's lifelikeness various schemata are mobilized and checked against this pre-existent world: some do not fit at all and are discarded; others fit in some ways though not in others, and must be worked on. Image-making is thought of here, in the words of Gombrich, as 'the gradual modification of the traditional schematic conventions of image-making under the pressure of novel demands' (Gombrich 1977: xi). First there is the vision, real or imaginary, that is to be represented; then there is the re-presentation, more or less accurate, of that original form.

I don't want here to list the various things which might be wrong with this account, but would like instead to move to the account which can most plausibly displace it, the semiological version in which image-making is thought of not as a secondary activity, reduplicating a prior world, but as an activity which together with other activities *makes* (rather than pictures) the world. A form of analysis emerges in which discursive or representational practices are found to *interact* with other (e.g. economic and political) practices and not just to *reflect* these; so that you can't simply read off a state of affairs in the social formation against its counterpart in art, but have to regard the image as involved in direct give-and-take with the rest of the social field with which it is, of course, continuous.[2]

I find this orientation better than the first one, but I am concerned about the viewpointing. The viewpoint which apprehends as interaction the struggle among all the economic, political, ideological, and signifying practices, the viewpoint which oversees this global state of affairs, is that of an always superior wisdom. Those who come later, as they look back, draw up the global map of practices which once struggled and contended within the social formation; yet for those inhabiting the social formation, as they inhabit it, such a panorama is exactly inaccessible. Since the material which the historian deals with always takes the form of traces, archives, marks of passage, conspectus is permanently available; all the historian needs is to view the traces all at once. It is the privilege of the latecomer to be able to gaze at the entire field of remains; but for those who live *in* history, such abstraction is clearly not possible. In the *durée* of history, all that is known directly is a local situation, one position only in the field of interactions, a point of knowledge hedged about by ignorance. Because the situation is actual and not recollected, because it is experienced in its passing and not experienced as the already-passed, this is necessarily a position of ignorance. Exactly because the experience is real, it is apprehended as a field in which some things are understood and others not.

There need be nothing wrong with global knowledge, in which all the factors discoverable in the remains are arrayed all at once. Most art history rightly commits itself to the viewpoint of a retrospective knowledge in which all the factors present in the original object are discovered as interaction. Yet the object of most art history, the image as it is made and as it is being made, does not in fact share that perspective. In a sense the perspective contained in the work is just the opposite: not that of knowledge, but exactly of ignorance.

Within the perspective of history as it is experienced, rather than as it might be posthumously reassembled, the feature I am calling ignorance is without content. In situations as we live them out, we not only cannot certainly know that *of which* we are ignorant; we cannot certainly know that we *are* ignorant. Ignorance presents itself not as something there before us, but as disturbance within what is before us. The field of situational experience and the field of historiography are therefore asymmetrical. To be sure, the historian may admit to his own kinds of ignorance and say, for example, that he or she cannot discover the whole truth. The historian may realize that some pieces of the jigsaw are lost forever. Yet this ought not to interfere with or invalidate the project – even if most of the pieces are lost in this way. The task is to lay out the pieces (the traces, the archive) in such a fashion that everything fits and the gaps, so far from being concealed, are also shown. But this viewpoint, of objectified knowledge, is the reverse of situational knowledge. There, what one is ignorant of remains *radically* unknown. One is presented with complete experience but the experience is not understood as complete. One has a jigsaw with all the pieces, but still the picture is indistinct.

What I am suggesting is that the ignorance of knowledge, incompleteness in the archive, is something quite different from the knowledge of ignorance, the form of knowing as it is lived out in actual situations: and art history is far likelier to embody the former than the latter. Like much 'academic' reasoning, it is apt to project into the object of knowledge the principle of its own relation to knowledge (see Bourdieu 1976: 2, 16–22). Seeking total knowledge (without gaps) it is prone to find in its object a total state (without gaps): the image interlocked with all the other practices (discursive, economic, political, etc.) in the social formation as a whole.

To counter such a projection let us attend to the mode of ignorance embodied in actual representations and experienced in actual time (*durée*). Such ignorance is not only the mark or symptom of the real: it is the mode in which the real actually manifests.

Some examples. In *Fear and Trembling*, Kierkegaard contrasts two sacrifices, that of Agamemnon sacrificing his daughter Iphigenia, and that of Abraham sacrificing his son Isaac (Kierkegaard 1939). Kierkegaard calls the sacrifice of Iphigenia teleological, in that Agamemnon makes his painful but rational decision knowing that Iphigenia's death is necessary to appease the god whose anger is preventing the Greek fleet from sailing. The sacrifice must take place if the Greeks are to advance and Troy is to be taken: it is an event directed towards an exact future, and oracles have predicted the outcome in advance. But the sacrifice of Isaac is the opposite of this; Kierkegaard calls it a 'teleological suspension'. Abraham does not know that at the last minute Isaac will be saved. His act is directed towards no rational goal or outcome: Abraham acts out of a pure present that does not know the future; the sacrifice is directed towards no specific goal or telos such as the fall of Troy; in this act of complete faith Abraham exactly screens from himself the future outcome, the consequences of murdering his own son for no reason men might understand. He performs his act in a temporality of sheer *durée*, a temporality in which action comes adrift from causes, since Abraham has no reason in worldly terms for killing Isaac, and comes adrift also from goals, since the action is performed without reference to a set of anticipated consequences. The story of Agamemnon's sacrifice presents no particular problem for narration, since it has its beginning (the becalming of the Greek fleet), its middle (the crisis in which Agamemnon finds himself), and its end (the Greek victory). This is the structure in which Agamemnon acts, and both origin and outcome direct his hand. But the story of Abraham's sacrifice poses for Kierkegaard enormous narrative difficulty. Agamemnon he understands, but he cannot understand Abraham, whose action exactly cannot be described in tragic terms to do with beginnings, middles, ends, or prefigured outcomes. For the historian, only the action of Agamemnon may make immediate sense, structured as it is by the same teleological temporality by which history is understood as a causal chain and historiography as a revealing of the track that guides action forward from state to state. The action of Abraham makes no reference to this temporality of narrative coherence; it unfolds in existential duration without reference to past or future.

A second example, by way of Gombrich: Giotto records the likeness of the human face. To do so he takes, then modifies, the scheme that comes to him from tradition: here and there the formula received from, say, Cimabue, needs to be altered. Is this to say that Giotto, as he surpasses Cimabue, is approximating – getting closer to – the real? Gombrich would certainly say so; yet the same facts can be interpreted in another way. The relation of representation to the real does not have to be thought of teleologically, as Gombrich does, or as the tendency towards an ideal Essential Copy. Rather, the real can be thought to manifest situationally, *in the interval* between Giotto and Cimabue, *as the distance* between the first schema and the second: in the gaps between the spokes, and as disturbances, turning and overturning of the contents of the representation, rather than as itself the *content* of representation.

A schema prevails, until something dislodges it. If reality is thought of as always mediated by cultural work (by signs) then it is *never* represented directly, and always manifests obliquely in this way, showing (so to speak) only its negative profile. And such a real can validate the term 'realist' just as forcefully as a reality immediately known. If the mark of the situationally real is an ignorance of the total field, and a *hypothetical* relation to actuality, then representation of that radical ignorance of Abraham carries as much lived actuality as Agamemnon's foreknowledge of Greek victory. Yet the bias of historical knowledge is to convert the hypothetical into the known; so that disturbance or incoherence in the image is considered *a problem to be overcome*, on the way to the image, rather than *a feature inherent within the image*.

Whether or not the incoherence in *Eylau* and *Jaffa* is to be overcome or respected, solved or retained, is in my view the principal question in both these paintings. But to state the case for 'retention' (rather than resolution) I need first to go back to David.

III

An important difference between *The Oath of the Horatii* (Fig. 3) and its precursors, J.-A. Beaufort's *The Oath of Brutus* (Fig. 4) and Gavin Hamilton's *Brutus* (Fig. 5) is that these earlier works clearly enact or describe the narratives they invoke (Rosenblum, 1961, 1970). Hamilton stays even closer to the Lucretia story than Beaufort. The story itself has two elements – the rape of Lucretia and then its aftermath, Brutus swearing to destroy the imperial house. Hamilton bonds both elements together round the dagger which has a part to play in each. Lucretia is presented as directly next to, so adjacent as to be the clear cause of, Brutus' oath of vengeance. Beaufort perhaps seems less eager to display the whole of the Lucretia narrative all at once, and separates the episodes spatially: Lucretia moves over to the left and no longer takes part in the scene; that first episode of the story is only touched on, while the second episode, the oath, is described in detail. Yet despite these differences, both Beaufort and Hamilton are doing the same thing: *illustrating* the complete narrative, in the sense of relaying it to the viewer directly and in full.

Now think of the *Horatii*. The story, like that of Lucretia, has a 'before' and an 'after'. The Romans and Albans have been warring, and a battle between representative warriors from each side is to decide the issue. After that battle, the one victorious Horatian brother will return and kill his sister, Camilla. Eventually his crime will be pardoned by the king. Yet this is not at all what we find *enacted* or *described* in *The Oath of the Horatii*. The image creates a scene not to be found in any of the literary sources.[3] In the invented scene we find all the elements of the story but not its diegesis; the components of the story, but not its action (in the mechanical sense). Instead of acting the narrative out, the image presents it in abstract guise, as the forces in the story rather than the events. What we see is at a distinct remove from the story we know: a sort of commentary or gloss on the story, a recapitulation or résumé. Because of this removal we are likelier to feel the force of the chiasmus *behind*

Figure 3. David, *The Oath of the Horatii*. Paris: Louvre.

the story – the strange symmetries of its design (Alba/Roma, Horatii/Curatii, brothers/sisters) – than the anecdotal unfolding of the story itself. The larger issues (gender relations and alienations, as well as contemporary political reverberations) will strike us more strongly than the detail of the narrative (which at this distance grows hazy, to say the least).

Seen from the viewpoint of narrative analysis, this sense of *removal* and *summation* is one of the painting's principal features. Interestingly, they are qualities also detectable in David's handling of his Poussin source. David takes from Poussin's *Sabines* (Louvre version; Fig. 6) two figures who, if we isolate them, similarly sum up the narrative in which they feature: King Romulus (who becomes Horatius; Figs 7 and 8) and the lictor (who becomes the nearest Horatian brother; Figs 9 and 10). Between them they recapitulate the salient features of the whole Sabine narrative, including the authorized character of the violence towards family and females. Romulus and the lictor condense into themselves, so to speak, the essential surrounding story and re-express it by synecdoche, simply by their postures. In the same way the swords in *The Oath of the Horatii* condense their surrounding narrative: they

Figure 4. Jacques-Antoine Beaufort, *The Oath of Brutus*. Nevers: Musée municipal.

Figure 5. Gavin Hamilton, *The Oath of Brutus*. London: Drury Lane Theatre.

Figure 6. Poussin, *The Rape of the Sabine Women*. Paris: Louvre.

Figure 7. Poussin, *The Rape of the Sabine Women* (detail, reversed).

Figure 8. David, *The Oath of the Horatii* (detail).

Figure 9. Poussin, *The Rape of the Sabine Women* (detail).

Figure 10. David, *The Oath of Horatii* (detail).

Figure 11. David, *The Death of Socrates*. New York: the Metropolitan Museum of Art.

Figure 12. David, *Brutus receiving the bodies of his sons*. Paris: Louvre.

Figure 13. P. A. Tardieu after David, *Lepelletier de Saint-Fargeau*. Paris: Bibliothè-que national.

stand for the whole story, yet curiously they do not belong to or enact the story itself.

The strategy of side-stepping the narrative, of taking the image *away* from the narrative, is hardly less striking in the *Socrates* (Fig. 11) and the *Brutus* (Fig. 12). David paints not the drinking of the hemlock, but the moment *before*, and *not* Brutus condemning his sons to death, but the return of their bodies. Avoiding or voiding the narratives, the image places itself at the margin of its text, and this margin in turn generates further margins; so that we find ourselves attending not to Brutus and his sons, but (in order of remoteness) their mother, sisters, nurse, and then the chairs, the still life on the table, the scissors, the wool, the basket. In the same way, we look not at Socrates and the hemlock, but the *têtes d'expression*, the scroll, the manacles, the lamp, the stand, the chipped surfaces of masonry. David's images here are centrifugal; they fly out from texts, seeking a margin where the text's influence will end. In that margin the spectator is inscribed. There, at the centre, the text and its reader; here, at the expanding edge, the image and its viewer. The still life of scissors, wool, and basket, or the shadow cast by a lamp-stand across broken masonry, are *for the viewer*; they propose and assume a viewer who exceeds the reader, and they advertise that this is what they are doing.

Figure 14. David, Versailles sketchbook, p. 24 verso and p. 25, Versailles.

Figure 15. David, Versailles sketchbook, p. 10 verso and p. 11, Versailles.

Indeed this seems to be the principal feature of word/image relations in David's histories up to 1789; the image distances itself from the text, establishes a relationship with it of synecdoche and abstraction, of marginality and flight. Out of this grows a space of *viewing* where the text can be regarded in essence and across a contemplative interval. Analysed in terms of an evolution from the 1780s into the 1790s, this creation of interval is then the basis for the creation of dialectic which follows after 1789. If David's pre-Revolutionary work opens up a space for the viewer across which to contemplate the text of his paintings, his Revolutionary works fill that contemplative space with dialectic, a dialectic which now participates openly in the contemporary historical field.

IV

Take, for example, the lost *Lepelletier* (Fig. 13). The viewer may be supposed to know the full story of Lepelletier's assassination, a central event in the Revolution. Lepelletier, a former courtier, had voted for the death of the king, and was later assassinated by counter-revolutionaries. The vote to execute Louis had passed with the slenderest majority, and Lepelletier's ballot paper is what we see in the image, transfixed by the sword. Yet the image exactly takes us out of that precisely local context by suppressing all the details. In place of the narrative, and in a sense to avoid the narrative, David gives us instead summary emblems. As in the *Horatii*, there is synecdoche – the sword and ballot paper are taken out of the actual narrative and made to sum it up; and at the same time there is abstraction – the emblems depict the forces of the narrative but not the events. The sword creates a distance from which viewing can then contemplate the assassination and assess its nature: it can be seen as the sword of regicide; it is also the sword of tyranny which always menaces freedom. In the contemplative interval opened up out of the narrative, David ranges the forces of politics and of history, and ranges them so that the viewer is requested or required to think about their presence in the representation. To the extent that it demands the participation of the viewer for its completion, the painting is more than simple propaganda. It so juxtaposes modernity and antiquity that, instead of thinking of neo-classicism as simply a style of decoration, the viewer must *think* about this proposed relation between antiquity and modernity. The relation is one of interrogation, rather than type/anti-type fulfilment. The inadequacies of the neo-classical style to the events of the Revolution are at least as telling as the parallels of Paris with Sparta or Republican Rome.

David himself is constantly jumping between the modern and the antique, and the Versailles sketchbook portrays the revolutionaries as Romans (Figs 14 and 15), but this is not so much an exercise in decorative style as a reflex of the

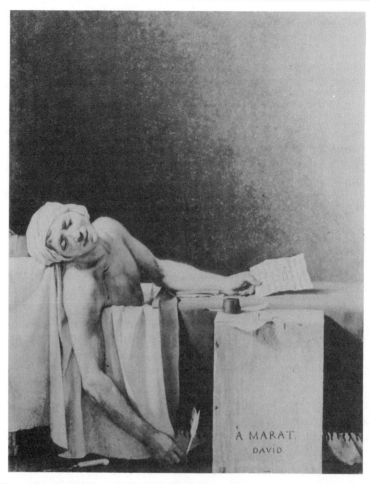

Figure 16. David, *Marat assassiné*. Brussels: Musées royaux des Beaux-Arts.

intellect, as the mind tries to assimilate the unprecedented, unimaginable, enormous events of the Revolution to the categories of the already-known. When Lepelletier is portrayed as a Trojan, as Hector, what appears is not Lepelletier *in the guise of* Hector so much as a montage of discourses, Troy against Paris, antiquity against modernity: not one dissolving into the other, as a consoling disguise or impersonation, but both fully arrayed in problematic distinctness and conjunction. Were the form of Lepelletier to melt into that of Hector, or the members of the National Assembly to dissolve into the shades of Romans, we would be in a much more stable world than David's Revolutionary work actually gives us. *Lepelletier* does not merge into Hector; the double iconography does not disappear, but remains foregrounded and unamenable. And to the degree that the double iconography stays double, it proposes and assumes a spectator whose understanding of the image will be active, critical, and dialectical.

This is even clearer in *Marat assassiné* (Fig. 16). Suppression of detail is extreme. Although David had visited Marat's apartment just before the assassination, and presumably could have supplied a surrounding *Umwelt* of the stablest kind, instead he reduces the narrative to those essential components which express, by synecdoche, the essential event without a demeaning descent into anecdote (Brookner 1980: 113–14). Each of the elements – the frugal packing case, the shroud-like sheet, the bath, the quill, the ink-stand – stands *for* the assassinated Marat; each element, considered in isolation, would summon the identification 'Marat!' by synecdoche. We are not in a real room or in normal physical space. Dislocated from actual space, the objects within the painting re-emerge in contemplative or subjective space, where they are famously transfigured.

Marat appears in the likeness of the dead Christ, in the fashion of a Deposition or Pietà. But although Christian iconography is invoked, it precisely does not exhaust the image. If it did, the Revolutionary work would be not only counter-Revolutionary but cloying. What saves it from such a fate is again its acute sense of dialectic. The secular Marat and the Christian Marat are placed in interactive relation, in the space of contemplative viewing which opens up in David when the anecdotal narrative is side-stepped. In this contemplative space we see side by side the sacred and the profane; the juxtaposition of Christ/Marat places the viewer in a dialectical field occupied by Christianity and dechristianization, in this era when the state breaks with Christian faith and Christian temporality (the canvas shows clearly that we are in year two of the republic). The painting interrogates each of these by means of its opposite. It precisely prevents one side of the dialectic from masking its antagonist: we do not feel that the image is 'really' Christian or 'really' non-Christian; it insists on the clear separation of terms.

V

David's sense of dialectic was already highly developed in the 1780s. The *Brutus* and *The Oath of the Horatii* opened on to a fully oppositional field in which woman and family, mercy and the individual are ranged against their antagonists: men, severity, and the state. The *Socrates* juxtaposes non-Christian and Christian frameworks in ways which make it the direct precursor of *Marat*; just like *Marat*, *Socrates* gives us a non-Christian martyrdom which is nevertheless suffused with ecclesiastical atmospherics –

Figure 17. Jean-Baptiste Regnault, *Liberty or Death*. Hamburg: Kunsthalle.

twelve disciples, a chalice, eucharistic hand gestures, and so forth. The figure
of Socrates had been of particular significance to Enlightenment thinkers,
since his life and death illustrated how far virtue could go in a pagan or
non-Christian framework: David finds a visual equivalent to this juxtaposition and its continuing interest (see Brookner 1980: 80). David's Revolutionary painting builds directly on this kind of achievement. *Lepelletier,
Marat*, and *Bara* go further in dispensing with narrative, and the dialectic is
now in touch with the actual centre of politics; yet the fundamental structure –
the side-stepping of story, the widening of contemplative interval, and the

filling of the interval with directly agonistic forces – is continuous with his production up to 1789.

What changes in the 1790s faster than David is the Parisian public. Modes of representation are no longer thought of as neutral, or simply as instrumental means to carry a content: representation is itself brought into the Revolution and subjected to its dialectic.[4] We have to think of the Parisian public, in the era of *Lepelletier* and *Marat*, as acutely aware of the symbolic charge of representations. People had experienced the renaming of the years, months, and days; the destruction of the old statues and the erection of new ones; the impact on the visual field of the Revolutionary pageants and the dechristianization programme; the renaming of cities, churches, institutions, individuals, streets, squares, and the faces in the pack of cards (Herbert 1972; and Dowd 1948).

Regnault's *Liberty or Death* (Fig. 17) grows directly out of such visual sophistication and critical alertness. It was destined for the Jacobin headquarters, in what had previously been the Cordeliers Church. Although the painting is so stridently an allegory, it forcefully overturns the customary stasis of allegorical representations. Under normal circumstances allegory is in fact the least dialectical of forms: x stands for y in a direct, one-to-one relation, with no possibility of altering or querying the structure. In the Regnault, normally static allegorical forms are radicalized and absorbed into the Revolutionary dialectic. Thus the central figure is *not*, in this dechristianized France, an archangel, any more than the destination of the painting is the Church of the Cordeliers, rather than the Jacobin Club. Whether the central winged figure represents the Revolution or the People is secondary to the primary force of the representation, which is to be *not* Michael, or Gabriel. The seated woman – Liberty, or the Republic – has since 1792 replaced the monarch as the official emblem of the state: she is *not-Louis*.[5] Jacobin iconography is built up from such negations: the triangle or level of quality is *not* the Eye of God; the red cap, once the sign of oppression and opposition, now stands for revolutionary victory; and despite the celestial *mise-en-scène* the grim reaper is not there to be transcended or to speak to us of salvation in another life.

Not even David in the *Marat* had pushed the dialectic of sacred and profane, or pre-Revolutionary and Revolutionary, as far as this; or pushed dialectic itself to the extremes evident here. If, in allegory, the viewer is usually proposed as passive before meaning, here the radicalization of allegory proposes a viewer who is, on the contrary, so actively productive of meaning as to become the virtual creator of the image. Each part of the allegory asks to be recognized as much under an implied mode of negation as in actual representation: the Revolution is not a guided messenger, death is not angelic, and no Eye of God watches over the scene.

VI

In David's work after Thermidor the radically dialectical quality of *Marat* and *Lepelletier* remains in force, notably in *The Intervention of the Sabine Women* (Fig. 18). After the rape of their women by the Romans, it took the Sabines three years to mount a counter-offensive, during which time their former sisters, daughters, and fiancées have become Roman wives and mothers, a fact which Hersilia (the central female figure) tries to demonstrate to the warring Romulus (on the right) and Tatius (the Sabine leader, on the left) (Brookner 1980).[6] David maps his classical story on to the dialectic of contemporary history through an adroit manipulation of pictorial detail.

The picture divides into roughly two camps, with the Romans on the right and the Sabines on the left. The identity of the Romans is confirmed by a number of minor, yet undeniable touches. Romulus bears on his shield a scene showing himself and Remus suckled by the she-wolf, beneath which we read the name ROMA. In terms of David's own painting, and the public recognition of its internal allusions, this points directly to the *Brutus* of 1789, where we see Romulus, Remus, and the wolf, carved into the pedestal of the state of Rome; David is taking up the thematic of state over family, and Romulus and the Romans are about to turn against the Sabine grandfathers and fathers-in-law. At the same time the stance of Romulus quotes directly from the principal brother in *The Oath of the Horatii*, the one who goes on to kill his sister Camilla in a burst of patriotic fervour.

Since the figure of Brutus had become, in the period from 1789 to 1794, an emblem of patriotic virtue, and *The Oath of the Horatii* had been similarly interpreted as a tribute to patriotic self-sacrifice, these allusions identify Romulus and the Romans as Revolutionaries, and specifically as Jacobins. This reading is confirmed if we look behind Romulus to the curious behaviour of hats and helmets. Notice first the strange rhyme between the helmet worn by the mounted warrior who is shown sheathing his sword, and the two helmets held aloft over Romulus' shield. Removing one's helmet, like putting one's sword back into its scabbard, marks a refusal to fight, and the mounted warrior and the helmets held aloft spell out the same idea, of truce. Now consider the Phrygian caps, and particularly these three: the cap worn by the figure whose face is partially hidden by the profile of a horse (the horse of the warrior who sheathes his sword); then the cap worn by the groom who leads a dark horse out of the right of the painting; and, finally, the empty cap held up on a spear above the head of Romulus. In the period of this painting, the Phrygian cap is still the cap of Liberty: imagery of the *bonnet rouge* had spread like wildfire from 1789 to 1794, as any visit to the Musée Carnavalet will prove. Yet to place the *bonnet rouge* on a spear and to hold it aloft does not, this time, figure the sans-culottes or the Jacobins, but exactly truce: the

Figure 18. David, *The Intervention of the Sabine Women*. Paris: Louvre.

ending of Jacobin fervour, and by the same token a political amnesty extended towards the 'terrorists' and erstwhile Jacobin supporters.

Against the force of Jacobinism, the picture marshals a dialectical counterforce, through an imagery of the family and private life. An ancient nurse (probably a portrait of David's own nurse) is about to bare her breast, to remind Romulus of his human origins and to oppose the power of the she-wolf (which we see raised high on a Roman standard at the right edge of the painting). Next to her kneels a young mother, a portrait this time of Aurore Bellegarde, the Directoire beauty who, in the season of the painting's first exhibition, tended to go to the theatre proudly sporting the same dishevelled coiffure David gives her here (Delécluze 1855: 214). The two standing women are perhaps even more interesting. Their movements are related: those of Hersilia at the centre of the picture, dressed in white, her arms extended in a gesture of reconciliation; and those of the woman who stands behind Hersilia, dressed in red, her hands turned in towards her head. If Hersilia's arm-gesture means reconciliation and harmony, the gesture of the woman behind her is the opposite of that, and signals conflict and discord. At the same time, her scarlet tunic is the strongest colour in the painting. It is at least possible that, if Hersilia represents the harmonies and amnesties of France under the Directoire, the scarlet figure behind her represents the previous era of bloody conflict, represents specifically the France of the Terror: if this is so, it would explain why her face is somewhat hidden or masked by her hands, by shadow, and by the scarlet cloak over her head. The whole picture concerns the transformation of Revolutionary bloodletting into Directoire reconciliation, and this involves forgiving and forgetting, the screening out of Jacobinism and of the Terror, and their resolution into the dove-white harmonies of Hersilia. Perhaps it is only by reading it as an allegory of Directoire society that we can fully understand the immense popularity of this painting in its period: crowds thronged into David's gallery in the Louvre to view it, paying to do so – with the proceeds David bought himself a property in the Seine-et-Marne. Its inner dialectic is that of pre-Thermidor and post-Thermidor: the dialectic of Directoire society itself, as the French lived out the contradiction between their Jacobin or Revolutionary legacy, and the conservatism of the reaction. Two perspectives meet in a dialectic which is the central political dialectic of the period of the *Sabines*.

Gros inherits from his master David a neo-classical aesthetic which he has to struggle against constantly. He also inherits David's acute sense of dialectic, and the articulation of dialectic with history lived out as a process in present or durational time. Both *Jaffa* and *Eylau* continue the series which runs back through the *Sabines*, *Marat*, *Lepelletier*, to the *Brutus* and the *Oath*. But there is a change in the way dialectic is handled. Contradiction between perspectives is stressed far more than in, for example, the *Sabines*, with its atmosphere of synthesis and reconciliation. In *Jaffa* two perspectives, instead of converging, diverge, to a degree which almost pulls the painting apart. Gros retains from David's *Socrates* and *Marat* the idea of a dialectic between sacred and profane, but the relation between these two perspectives now borders on the fissile, and on incoherence.

VII

Seen in a secular perspective, the whole episode in the plague-house conveys victorious rationality and objectivity.[7] As the *livret* puts it: 'Pour éloigner davantage l'effrayante idée d'une contagion subite et incurable, [Napoléon] fit ouvrir devant lui quelques tumeurs péstilentielles et en toucha plusieurs.'[8] Napoleon touches the *pestiféré* in order to restore troop morale. He had noticed during the course of the Egyptian campaign that 'c'est une des circonstances particulières de la peste qu'elle est plus dangereuse pour les personnes qui la craignent' (Napoleon 1847): he observed that the people who were most frightened of the plague tended to be the very ones who most easily succumbed to it; and his gesture of touching the *pestiféré* is a way of allaying such imaginary fears. The whole import of the gesture is rationalistic: it is designed to counter the demons of fearful imagination and panicking subjectivity.

What is interesting is that the rationality which is dramatized in *Jaffa* is therefore strangely compromised. It does not want to banish phantasms and fears but rather to manipulate these, and to arouse and exploit the irrational for purposes of its own. There is a strong sense of shadiness in a faculty which would act in this fashion. Yet the alternative seems equally problematic.

At the same time that he stresses victorious rationality, Gros also activates another perspective, an irrational perspective in which Napoleon appears as a mysteriously sacred figure. The rationalist gesture is now refracted across the same excitable imagination it officially subdues. Transfigured by the very faculty his gesture seeks to counter, the image of Napoleon grows numinous. Gros' complex and allusive second iconography presents the emperor in a number of sacred roles: as Saint Louis, the crusader king who visited and touched the sick in the pest-houses of North Africa, the king whose touch can heal (Friedlander 1940–1). Religious connotations abound. Besides Saint Louis, the image echoes the New Testament, and Napoleon stands before the *pestiféré* as Christ before Lazarus. An intercessor against plague, he is also Saint Roch (perhaps specifically the Saint Roch of David, from whom Gros may be taking the idea of the exhausted, naked giant). A further resonance is distinctly apocalyptic. The despairing man seated to the left of the painting is directly quoted from the Sistine Chapel, and this detail serves to confirm that the gigantic plague-victim is also Michelangelesque, a figure, in fact, from the Last Judgement. It is typical of the blurring resonances of the painting's iconography that the association with the Last Judgement in no way contradicts the further suggestion, of a secular harrowing of Hell.

The problem is that such religious allusions seem unstoppable. At the other end of the spectrum from rationalism, the aroused imagination multiplies analogies and connotations in a way which suggests a final absence of control. One can follow at least the coherence of Napoleon seen as Saint Louis, as Saint Roch, as Christ, but this is by no means where the resonances end. The *pestiféré* sufficiently resembles a Deposition for the image to begin to shift its centre and to suggest the plague-victim – not the emperor – as Christ (Fig. 19). Once this happens it is only a step further to see Napoleon as an attendant figure, such as Joseph of Arimathea; and, finally, as he pokes his finger into the wounds, as Saint Thomas investigating the stigmata. The religious imagination is pushed to a point where it is found infinitely excitable, and suggestible, and therefore an appropriate counterpart for cynical or manipulative rationalism.

Again, with *The Field of Eylau* one is acutely conscious of polarization causing disturbance, incoherence, in the iconography.[9] *Eylau* looks back to

Figure 19. Gros, *The Plague-House at Jaffa* (detail).

Jaffa, and to *Marat* and *Socrates*, yet the sacred/secular dialectic is now the end of its development. Whereas in *Jaffa* the mythopoetic resonances suggested an imagination feverishly active, in *Eylau* the resonances are automatic and inert. A discourse of the sacred presents Napoleon as a holy emperor, whose hand-gesture of benediction blesses the battlefield and whose ascensional gaze calls on heavenly powers. The flattened frieze-like area round him has the archaic character of sacred representations, and functions as a hieratic space in which the contact of heaven and earth may occur. Beyond this central space are the worshippers, notably the cossack who kneels to receive the imperial blessing. The influence of the sacred does not end here, but passes outwards to the bodies of the dead, hallowing the bodies and reordering their unshriven disorder, as though Napoleon's ritual gestures performed an essential ceremony of burial or consecration.

Against this heightened iconography of sacredness Gros places his alternative account, which speaks only of material death (Fig. 20). The corpses, colossally enlarged, dominate the eye-level space of actual viewing, and serve to relegate the hieratic emperor to a distance where he and his generals appear remote, theatrical, and irrelevant. The corpses are seen objectively, as if not symbolized at all, and indeed medical vision is placed close to the spectator, who at eye level confronts the gaze not of Napoleon but of the army surgeons.[10] From this perspective the gestures of the emperor are an empty

Figure 20. Gros, *The Battlefield of Eylau* (detail).

rigmarole, and the sacred allusions appear as the mere reflex of an imagination working on automatic pathways.

Such polarization almost pulls the image apart, and *Eylau* is certainly the most agonized of the works in its tradition. But keeping the tension of the dialectic fully in view, and preserving it fully *in* tension, are tasks which may be difficult to carry out in the normal framework of historical knowledge. There are a number of ways in which *Jaffa* and *Eylau* can be invisibly closed down and normalized. Both are propaganda pieces, and in both cases the commission can be thought of as motivated by the need to cover up some ugly alternative versions of the events: for instance, the rumour that Napoleon had ordered to be poisoned those of his troops who were too sick to rejoin the Egyptian army, or the fact that the battle of Eylau could be seen as expensive defeat. It is not difficult to find documentary evidence to account for what seems like Gros' disaffection with Napoleon; and once the documents are on the table it cannot be long before the explanation is complete. Such explanation is necessarily reductive, not because it has got hold of the wrong documents but because it is an *explanation*; that is, the projection of knowledge into the existential field of ignorance. Projecting into the object of knowledge the principle of its own relation to knowledge, explanation finds a total field (without gaps), a narrative, a story. The tradition we are dealing with characteristically side-steps narrative, and for good reason: narrative can be the denial, as dialectic can be the acknowledgement, of art's existential roots.

The risk of reading the iconographic disturbances in *Jaffa* and *Eylau* as problems to be solved on the way to the image, rather than as inherent and irreducible features of the image, is that these paintings, together with Regnault's *Liberty or Death*, the *Marat, Lepelletier*, and even *Socrates*, may lose their realism, in the sense I outlined earlier. Together they form a tradition which is, I suggest, radically dialectical. The *Socrates* of David does not tell you which perspective rules the image, pagan or Christian: it opens up an interval, away from the narrative, in which the two discourses can precisely engage in struggle; and it is the same with the others. Yet a non-dialectical art history may find it difficult to understand that process as process, and will want instead to make of the painting the illustration of its own explanatory narrative, and seek its own reflection in the image. It will feel that the image, like itself, abstracts from the multiplicity of experiences a pure product, freed from the existential roots of knowledge. It will credit the image with a power, which it desires for itself, to reduce reality to a prospect that can be mastered *im Augenblick*. It presupposes a world which is constructed, elaborated, self-sufficient, reduced to significant contours and outlines – in a word, narrated – and not one 'which has been sent sprawling before us, to take or leave' (Barthes 1972: 256).

The tradition of dialectical painting which I have been sketching exactly frustrates such assumptions. It seeks, on the contrary, to modify representations by rendering them provisional and incomplete. It wants the image hollowed out, so that it can make no claim to contain or fix the world: it wants representation instead to unfix and *question* the world. This tradition has an acute sense of duration, and it resists the conversion of that duration into the mere oriented and meaningful *past* of historiography. Aware that actuality can all too readily be reduced to mere signs, it assaults the signs in the name of a real which is sensed, preserved, and respected only in disorder, and refuses to conceal or do away with the ignorance and the solitude of the existence which actually inhabits the real, the unassimilable world.

VIII

Let us review the stages the present discussion has passed through. We observed that in David's pre-Revolutionary paintings there is a tendency to side-step the narrative and to locate the image at a certain remove from textuality. Instead of giving us the story directly, David prefers to give a gloss or meditation on the story. In the *Brutus* and *The Oath of the Horatii* the forces within the narrative are abstracted and polarized in such a way that the viewer becomes an active interpreter dealing with a problematic of forces, rather than a passive observer receiving a familiar text. In David's Revolutionary work the image opens on to historical processes, instead of legends or myth, and the means of representation are foregrounded and participate in historical questions directly. The *Lepelletier* sets up a dialogue between antique and modern styles, the *Marat* sets up a dialogue between Christian and post-Christian frameworks, the *Sabines* sets up a dialogue between pre-Thermidorean and post-Thermidorean perspectives. These polarities operate simultaneously in such a way as to create an open rather than a closed visual text, a text which directly participates in the dialectic of historical process. Gros' *Jaffa* and *Eylau*, I suggest, retain this structure of dialectical openness, but now the distance between the frameworks or voices – crudely described as sacred and profane – is so great as to produce a radically disjunctive text, an open text in which the synthesis of contradictory frames or voices seems impossible. By the same token, the historical process plotted in this disjunctively dialogical fashion is presented as unamenable to synoptic understanding. Gros' paintings come from a history lived out as a present riven with contradiction. And my claim here is that art historical narrative, in so far as its method commits itself to the elimination of contradiction in favour of retrospective order, may not easily do justice to an imagery whose commitment lies in the opposite direction, working against synthesis, mediation, and the aoristic clarity which historical narrative demands.

One might finally reflect on the kind of 'theoretical object' I believe we are dealing with in these works of Gros. It is paradoxical. The claim that these paintings refuse interpretative clarity is itself being advanced as an interpretation. With one hand the possibility of synoptic interpretation is taken away, and with the other the unavailability of interpretation is proffered *as* the interpretation. How does one view this paradox?

One resolution is to locate two different temporalities: that of a radical *durée*, in which the principal feature is contradiction or incoherence; and that of an aoristic overview, in which the principal feature is retroactive order. We could name these as the temporalities of Abraham and Agamemnon, respectively. The point of the distinction would be that the act of viewing itself participates in both temporalities at once. If we isolate notional 'moments of viewing' we find they are penetrated by these conflicting temporalities all the time. Viewing travels forward into a future it does not know in advance. As we move with our eyes from one point of an image to another, we are so to speak in the position of Abraham: we are up against a force which may in the next moment overturn everything we have thought about the image so far.

Suddenly we encounter what eludes the visual schemata we have been using, a principle which Lacan (1979: 53–64) calls 'tuché' and Gombrich (1974) calls the moment of testing visual hypotheses. At the moment when a hypothesis breaks down, both past and future become unavailable as support to our viewing. Vision now inhabits a radical *durée* which cannot find synoptic order in the visual field. But this temporality of *durée*, of Abraham, exists side by side with and is penetrated by a temporality of aoristic order, an Agamemnon-like awareness which holds past, present, and future in a single frame. It is this second temporality, I suggest, which tends to govern art historical narrative. Against that aoristic order I am not, in fact, asserting some primacy of radical *durée*, whether in historical or perceptual process. Rather, my suggestion is that in thinking and writing about paintings, and when we look at them, we open our awareness to the existence of both these temporalities which interpenetrate and cross our viewing of pictures. Painting itself may emphasize now one temporality and now the other. The paintings by Gros do, I think, activate a radical duration, but I would not want to suggest they activate it exclusively. I do not know what this would mean. But a criticism which would close down on that *durée* would, I think, to some extent be misrepresenting the paintings; even though the *demonstration* of that *durée* is something criticism may not be able to achieve. In so far as critical writing participates in aoristic or Agamemnon time, it cannot capture that other, Abraham-like time, of durational process. It can only point towards it; but in the case of Gros, this is something I believe it must try to do.

King's College, Cambridge

NOTES

1 On Gros' relations with David, see Delestre (1867) and Tripier Le Franc (1880).

2 On the interaction of representational practice with other social practices, see Mukarovsky (1976), Clark (1985: esp. 3–22), and Crow (1985).

3 On David's use of Corneille, see Brookner (1980: 70–7).

4 The degree to which David's paintings may be 'charged' with political meaning remains a matter of (intense) debate: see, in particular, Korshak (1987: 102–16; and Crow (1985), especially his concluding chapter.

5 On the figure of the Republic, see Agulhon (1981).

6 On pictorial representation of the Sabine women, see Bryson (1986).

7 See Fyjis-Walker (1984: esp. 68–124), and Lelièvre (1936: 289–304).

8 *Explication des ouvrages de Peinture, Sculpture, Architecture et Gravure exposés* . . . (Paris, 1804: 39–40).

9 Such incoherence is notably absent from other official representations of Eylau, of which the most interesting is the version by Charles Meynier (see Zieseniss 1960).

The circumstances of commission surrounding the Eylau paintings are outlined in Lelièvre (1953).

10 Reproduction cannot do justice to the facts of scale in this case: the foreground figures, perpendicular to the viewer's gaze, are 'undisturbed', but the figures of Napoleon and his generals are subject to a massive 'tilt' which, to be rectified, requires the viewer exactly to break away from the grip of the foreground and retire to a safe, panoptic distance.

BIBLIOGRAPHY

Agulhon (1981) *Marianne into Battle: Republican Imagery and Symbolism in France 1789–1880*, trans. J. Lloyd, Cambridge: Cambridge University Press.

Barthes, R. (1972) *Le degré zéro de l'écriture* (2nd edn), Paris: Editions du Seuil.

Bloom, Harold (1975) *The Anxiety of Influence: A Theory of Poetry*, New York: Oxford University Press.

Bourdieu, P. (1976) *Outline of a Theory of Practice*, trans. R. Nice, Cambridge: Cambridge University Press.

Brookner, A. (1980) *Jacques-Louis David*, London: Chatto & Windus.

Bryson, N. (1986) 'Two narratives of rape in the visual arts', in S. Tomaselli and R. Porter (eds), *Rape*, Oxford: Basil Blackwell.

Clark, T. J. (1985) *The Painting of Modern Life: Paris in the Art of Manet and his Followers*, London: Thames & Hudson.

Crow, T. (1985) *Painters and Public Life in Eighteenth-Century Paris*, New Haven and London: Yale University Press.

Delécluze, M. E. J. (1855) *Louis David: son école et son temps*, Paris: Didier.

Delestre, J. B. (1867) *Gros, sa vie et ses ouvrages* (2nd edn), Paris.

Dowd, D. L. (1948) *J. L. David: Pageant-Master of the Republic*, Lincoln, Nebr.: University of Nebraska Press.

Friedlander, W. (1940–1) 'Napoleon as "Roi Thaumaturge"', *Journal of the Warburg and Courtauld Institutes*.

Fyjis-Walker, Alexander (1984) 'Uses of iconography around 1804', (MPhil thesis, Courtauld Institute).

Gombrich, E. H. (1974) *The Sense of Order: A Study in the Psychology of Decorative Art*, London: Phaidon.

Gombrich, E. H. (1977) *Art and Illusion: A Study in the Psychology of Pictorial Representation* (5th edn), London: Phaidon.

Herbert, R. L. (1972) *David: Brutus*, London: Allen Lane.

Kerkegaard, S. (1939) *Fear and Trembling*, Oxford: Oxford University Press.

Korshak, Y. (1987) '*Paris and Helen* by Jacques-Louis David: choice and judgement on the eve of the French Revolution', *Art Bulletin*, LXIX, number 1 (March).

Lacan, J. (1979) 'Tuché and Automaton', in J. A. Miller (ed.), *The Four Fundamental Concepts of Psycho-Analysis*, trans. A. Sheridan, London: Penguin Books.

Lee, V. (1969) 'Jacques-Louis David: the Versailles sketchbook', *Burlington Magazine*, CXI, 197–208, 360–9.

Lelièvre, P. (1936) 'Gros, peintre d'histoire', *Gazette des Beaux-Arts*.

Lelièvre, P. (1953) 'Napoléon sur le champ de bataille d'Eylau: précisions sur les conditions de la commande', *Bulletin de la Société de l'Histoire de l'art français*, 69–75.

Mukarovsky, J. (1976) 'Art as semiological fact', *20th Century Studies* 15/16, 6–11.

Napoleon, (1847) *Campagnes d'Egypte et de Syrie 1789–1799*, ed. Bertrand, Paris, t.11, 52–3.

Rosenblum, R. (1961) 'Gavin Hamilton's *Brutus*', *Burlington Magazine*, CIII (January), 8–16.

Rosenblum, R. (1970) 'A source for David's *Horatii*', *Burlington Magazine*, CXII (May), 169–73.

Tripier Le Franc, J. (1880) *Histoire de la vie et de la mort du Baron Gros*, Paris.

Zieseniss, C. O. (1960) 'Napoléon à Eylau, une esquisse de Charles Meynier', *Revue des Arts*, 213–20.

New developments in realist philosophy

WILLIAM OUTHWAITE

Roy Bhaskar, *Scientific Realism and Human Emancipation*
London: Verso, 1986; hardback £29.95, paper £9.95; 308 pp.

Rom Harré, *Varieties of Realism: A Rationale for the Natural Sciences*
Oxford: Basil Blackwell, 1986; £25.00; viii + 375 pp.

Joseph Margolis, *Pragmatism Without Foundations: Reconciling Realism and Relativism*
Oxford: Basil Blackwell, 1986; £25.00; xix + 320 pp.

The philosophy of science is relevant to the history of the human sciences in at least three different ways. First, philosophy continues to function as a legitimating instance for knowledge in general and science (and the individual sciences) in particular; a role variously characterized as the self-consciousness of science at one pole, and a kind of thought-police of science at the other – with metaphors such as that of the super-ego located somewhere in between. Historians of science may not, and probably should not, want to take at face value such claims for philosophy in the various forms in which they have historically been made – but they cannot avoid taking them seriously as features of the culture of the sciences.

Second, there is the relationship between philosophy of science and history of science – a relationship symbolized for the past twenty-five years by the work of Thomas Kuhn. It is clear that Kuhn massively shifted the balance in this relationship from philosophy to history; philosophy of science can hardly any longer be conducted in isolation from the history of science. But if philosophy of science without history of science is empty, it remains to be seen whether the other side of the equation is equally valid: that history of science without philosophy of science is blind.

Finally, the historian of the human sciences can hardly fail to address the question of the status of these sciences as sciences, and *this* question, since at least the nineteenth century, has for better or worse been posed in the form of holding up the human and social sciences to a methodological ideal allegedly represented by the physics and the other sciences of nature. Once again, the historian of science may wish to avoid taking a stand on the *quid juris* implied by these procedures, but he or she cannot ignore the fact that this is the way in which the nature of the human sciences has historically been analysed.

The authors of the three books discussed here exemplify the close relationship between philosophy of science and the history and current practice of the individual sciences. Of the three, Margolis is probably nearest to a philosopher's philosopher, though one with a wide range of substantive interests. His book contains a powerful plea for the kind of philosophy of science which engages in detail with the history of individual sciences, as opposed to a more traditional kind of analytic epistemology which 'so often risks being empty and uncompelling (even at times irrelevant) in contrast to the more historical and problem-oriented methodology of current theories of science'.[1] For their part, Harré's and Bhaskar's routes into the philosophy of sciences were via a critical examination of the practice of the social sciences – behaviouristic social psychology for Harré, and various types of positivistic social and economic theory for Bhaskar. Although Harré's present book is concerned primarily with the natural sciences, he has also produced a vast quantity of work within social psychology. Bhaskar's second book, *The Possibility of Naturalism*, examined the implications for the social and human sciences of the position he had earlier presented in *A Realist Theory of Science*; the first two chapters of the volume develop some themes arising from these two books, while the third chapter maps out a general critique of positivist philosophy of science.

All three authors are committed, in their different ways, to what is known as a 'realist' position in the philosophy of science. The term realism has of course a long history, and like most, perhaps all, philosophical positions can only be understood in terms of what it is opposed to. Thus realism has been opposed to nominalism in theories of universals or general terms, and opposed to idealism or phenomenalism in the analysis of perception. More recently, 'scientific realism' has come to denote the position that the entities referred to in successful scientific theories may actually exist (at least at some level of description) and/or that successful scientific theories are true if they correspond (in some sense of this term) to actually existing states of affairs. A classic expression of this position is the one provided by W. F. Sellars, who held that elementary particles, for example, are actually more real than the objects of common-sense descriptions in ordinary language.

Modern realism is distinguished by its opposition to positivistic empiricism, on the one hand, and to what Bhaskar has come to call super-idealism on the other. Against empiricism's invocation of brute facts of experience, realism insists on the need for complex theoretical redescriptions of reality. Against super-idealism, realists deny that, in Kuhn's notorious phrase, scientists operating within different theoretical frameworks occupy different worlds. In the terms of classical philosophy, the realist position is that we 'constitute' the word epistemically, but its ontological constitution or make-up is independent of our conceptualization. As Bhaskar put it at the end of *A Realist Theory of Science* (2nd edn, p. 250): 'Things exist and act independently of our descriptions, but we can know them only under particular descriptions.'

Bhaskar's position is, however, somewhat unusual, in combining the very strong ontological thesis just quoted with extreme caution in respect to any particular scientific statements. He distinguishes between a philosophical ontology, which states merely that the world is differentiated, stratified, and is made up of relatively enduring structures and entities, and the ontologies of the various sciences which include, for example, alpha particles or radioactive decay. The status of the latter is a matter for physics, not philosophy.

This issue of scientific ontologies will be discussed later, in relation to Harré's book. For the moment it is enough to note the difference between Bhaskar's position and those of American philosophers such as Hilary Putnam, whose discussion of realism has been cast more in terms of epistemology and semantic notions such as truth and reference.

Associated with this internal difference between the two programmes is a certain difference in their orientation. Bhaskar, as noted above, has been concerned to move from the analysis of the natural sciences to the social domain, and it is a particular feature of the so-called 'new realism' in the UK that its leading exponents, like Bhaskar, have generally worked within the social sciences. Bhaskar's book of 1975 was parallelled, in the same year, by Russell Keat and John Urry's very influential *Social Theory as Science*, prefigured by an article by Keat in 1971; in 1977 Ted Benton published a book along similar lines, *The Philosophical Foundations of the Three Sociologies*. As it happens, these four writers were also strongly sympathetic to Marxist social theory, and their identification of Marx's own metatheory as realist was underpinned, in 1979, by Derek Sayer's book *Marx's Method*. The epistemological and semantic variant of realism, by contrast, was developed in a more purely philosophical climate.

Furthermore, there was a difference in the forms of argumentation used to support realism. Whereas Putnam tried to justify the realism he upheld in the early 1970s by a meta-induction from the success and broad convergence of modern scientific theories, Bhaskar advanced a more global transcendental argument from the very possibility of science. For Bhaskar, science in general and experimentation in particular is only possible or meaningful if the world exists in a structured way independently of our descriptions of it. In other words, the preconditions of science include not just human experience, as stressed by empiricism, and creative theorization, emphasized by transcendental idealist theories from Kant onwards, but a set of facts about the world – a world which, after all, existed much as it does now before human beings evolved and *a fortiori* before they began to do science.

Before passing on to realist accounts of the social sciences, we need to note a further essential feature of Harré's and Bhaskar's realism: their account of causal relations. As against the long-dominant Humean conception that these may be analysed as constant conjunctions of observed events, Harré and Madden, in *Causal Powers*, returned to an earlier tradition which analysed causality as a result of the powers and liabilities of things, and Bhaskar stressed the distinctiveness of the three domains of the real, the actual (events), and the empirical (experiences). Constant conjunctions at the actual level, or their observation, at the empirical level, were neither necessary nor sufficient to establish causal relations. Causal tendencies may neutralize each other such that there is no change to be observed, but the tendencies are no less real. What were the implications of these realist positions for the analysis of the human sciences? As noted above, the natural sciences had formed the initial basis for realist argumentation, and the British realists diverged on the question of the applicability of this programme to the social world. As we saw, Bhaskar, Keat and Urry, and Benton argued for the naturalistic view that the methods of the two sorts of science were broadly comparable, while Harré has continued to stress the distinctiveness of the social sciences and has upheld a conception of social psychology close to symbolic interactionism and ethnomethodology.[2]

The naturalists, too, have disagreed over just what modification needed to be made in the application of realist philosophy of science to the social domain. Bhaskar argued, in *The Possibility of Naturalism*, that social facts were concept-dependent, in the sense that they presupposed that social actors had some concept of what they were doing, activity-dependent, in that they existed only in and through individual or collective action and, unlike many natural structures, were only relatively enduring. Benton argued that this was to bend over too far towards an anti-naturalism, and that the differences between the natural and the social sciences were not after all so great – especially if one paid more attention than Bhaskar had done to the intermediate status of biology between the two extremes of physics on the one hand and, say, sociology on the other. While accepting the latter point I feel, if anything, more anxious than Bhaskar about discussing the ontological status of, say, social structures, as though the question of their existence or non-existence was as clear-cut (however difficult to determine) as that of most physical entities.

Rom Harré's book is therefore of particular interest, since it tackles head-on the issue of the ontologies of sciences of different kinds. Harré urges that we should abandon the elaborate redefinition of science offered by much philosophy and adopt instead a 'modest' policy realism concerned with the referents of theoretical terms rather than absolutist conceptions of truth.

> Taken in a policy way, referential realism amounts to the advice 'If a substantive term seems to denote a being of a certain natural kind (and some special conditions are satisfied by the theory in which that term functions) it is worth setting up a search for that being.' (p. 59; cf. pp. 67f.)

Theories, Harré suggests, must be differentiated into three rough types. Type 1 theories are concerned with the classification, prediction, etc., of observable phenomena.

> The referents of type 1 theories belong in Realm 1, the realm of actual and possible objects of experience. The moon and Pluto, the Grand Canyon and the Atlantic trench, the tongue and the renal portal vein belong in Realm 1. (p. 72)

Type 2 theories invoke a second realm of being whose objects are contingently unobservable but could/can be observed, given the right equipment. 'Micro-organisms, capillaries and X-ray stars belong in Realm 2' (ibid.). Such theories make up 'the vast majority of scientific theories' (p. 71); they involve the representation of a system which has not yet been observed.

> For type 3 theories we, the users, are committed, not only to the ontologies of Realm 1 and Realm 2, but also to beings which, if real, could not become phenomena for human observers, however well equipped with devices to amplify and extend the senses. Realm 3 is a domain of being beyond all possible experience. Quantum states, naked singularities, social structure and Freudian complexes are amongst the typical denizens of Realm 3. (p. 73)

The greater part of Harré's book is a stupendously detailed and wide-ranging account of the search-and-find procedures implied by scientific theories of these first two types. In Realm 3, he concedes, the criteria can *ex hypothesi* be only causal and not observational – leaving open, one hopes, for a future book, the question of the status of theoretical terms in the social sciences.

The present book is probably somewhat too detailed and technical for non-specialist readers, but it is a major work which should influence future thinking on these issues.

Bhaskar's two earlier books have already been mentioned. The first two chapters of the present book 'consolidate and develop' (preface) these arguments. They are, however, a good deal more than a restatement of these positions, and mark a shift in Bhaskar's work towards a yet deeper level of sophistication, of which the outward sign is further terminological innovation. Because of these complexities, I shall concentrate on just two themes in the book; the concept of emancipation and the critique of positivism.

Although it is surprisingly common for philosophies of science to be linked up with considerations of moral and political philosophy, whether liberal in the case of Popper or libertarian-anarchist in the case of Feyerabend, the connection between realism and emancipation is not a prima-facie one. It might reasonably be supposed that conventionalist theories of science are more obviously linked to emancipation, in the sense that, to put it somewhat caricaturally, we can make what we will of both the natural and the social world. Bhaskar's argument, in a nutshell, is that we require a conception of independently existing, natural and social structures (a) to sustain the concept of *critique* and (b) to ground meaningful projects of emancipation, conceived in terms of 'the transformation of structures, not the alteration or amelioration of states of affairs' (p. 171).

Any natural scientific theory is implicitly critical of alternative theories; social theories, moreover, may incorporate an explanatory critique of the social situations which have led to a misrecognition, in common sense and/or in competing theories, of those social situations. Marx's critique of political economy is the classic example of this. Positivism, by contrast, with its flat ontology of the world-as-experienced, postulates 'a derealized reality and a desocialized science' (p. 252). And, moreover, a desocialized society:

> In perfect resonance with the positivist concept of science as a behavioural response to the stimulus of given facts and their conjunctions, society is conceived as composed of individuals, motivated by given desires and conjoined (if at all) by contrast. (p. 287)

It is in this sense that positivism may be said to be 'the house-philosophy of the bourgeoisie' (p. 308).

Once again, the complexity of Bhaskar's arguments in the third chapter of his book, 'The positivist illusion', defies an adequate summary here, but the model which he develops is enormously rich and suggestive, and could inspire a large body of work in the history of ideas.

Margolis sets the terms of his book in a splendid first sentence which could serve as the motto for this review: 'We cannot seriously believe that science utterly misrepresents the way the world is; and we cannot accurately determine the fit between the two' (p. 1). He then goes on to map out, in a meticulous yet reasonably approachable manner, a set of paths through some existing realist and anti-realist positions. This is a valuable service, and makes the book an important addition to the literature, but readers on this side of the Atlantic are likely to find it somewhat disappointing. His itinerary parallels in many ways that framed by Bhaskar, following Harré, in 1975, and it is illustrative of the gap between British and American discussion of realism that he makes no reference to either of these writers, nor to Harré's American co-author Ed Madden. Even Mary Hesse, who played a very important part in the early development of British 'new realism' and is, I would think, also quite well known in North America, receives only a single insubstantial mention. Realists like myself in the Harré/Bhaskar mould will be encouraged to see someone arriving at a position close to theirs by a different route, but will not find much that is new or exciting.

Conversely, on the issue of relativism he is something of a sheep in wolf's clothing. Both the title and the subtitle of the book suggest something rather exhilarating and dangerous, whereas in fact Margolis is merely arguing, in a way which parallels that of Harré and Bhaskar, that we will often, for good reasons, not wish to ascribe simple truth or falsity to scientific theories, but rather to make more complex judgements such as 'a reasonable approximation within certain boundary conditions' and so forth. This moderate relativism, a position close to what Bhaskar calls epistemic relativism, is far from the more robust form represented by David Bloor and Barry Barnes, which Margolis does discuss at some length and rejects.[3] Similarly, Margolis's pragmatism and his rejection of foundationalism are close to the spirit of Harré's critique of 'truth realism' and a far cry from the sort of position upheld by Richard Rorty.

It will be seen, I hope, that these three books, despite their dissimilarities in subject-matter and orientation, map out a roughly congruent way of approaching the concept of science, along lines which cannot be without interest to historians of sciences which operate at the intersection of the pursuit of truth and a variety of moral and political concerns. A realist metatheory will not, of itself, resolve substantive questions in either of these spheres, but it constitutes, in my view, an essential precondition for posing these issues in an adequate manner.

Sussex University

NOTES

1 Margolis, pp. 152f. The quoted passage continues: 'Without taking sides on the issues raised respectively in the two domains, one sees at once the distinct difference in relevance, for realist questions, of the epistemological reflections, say, of such authors as Quine, Lehrer, and Fred Dretske, on the one hand, and Kuhn, van Fraassen, Cartwright, and Ian Hacking, on the other.'

2 As he disarmingly puts it in *Social Being* (Blackwell, 1979) p. 232: 'Realists in social science hold, and I would share their belief, that there are global patterns in the behaviour of men in groups, though as I have argued we have no adequate inductive method for finding them out.'

3 Barnes, in an unpublished paper delivered to a conference on *Realism in the Human Sciences* in 1986, has argued that his relativism is compatible with Bhaskar's realism, but the two seem to me to be far apart in their overall attitude to science.

The shaping of modern psychology and the framing of historical accounts

ROB FARR

L. S. Hearnshaw, *The Shaping of Modern Psychology: An historical introduction*
London: Routledge & Kegan Paul, 1987; hardback £19.95; viii + 423 pp.

The author of this stimulating volume is a distinguished scholar and educator who retired, in 1975, from the Chair of Psychology at the University of Liverpool. It is based on a series of lectures he gave at the University of Western Australia in the year following his retirement. In the interim between delivering the lectures and publishing the book Professor Hearnshaw completed and published his widely acclaimed biography of Burt (Hearnshaw 1979).

The book, as its title suggests, is a historical introduction to modern psychology. Hearnshaw agrees with Beloff (1973) that modern psychology is 'not a single unified science, but . . . a collection of more or less loosely affiliated disciplines each with its own peculiar concepts and laws, its own methods and techniques' (p. 221). It is, therefore, quite a daunting task to trace the historical antecedents of such a medley of subdisciplines. Hearnshaw achieves this by reviewing developments in a number of neighbouring disciplines. In chapter eight, for example, he traces the impact, on the development of psychology, of advances in the life sciences during the eighteenth and nineteenth centuries. In chapters ten and eleven he looks, respectively, at the influences of medicine and of the social sciences on the development of psychology. In chapter thirteen he traces developments in philosophy that have occurred since psychology gained its independence from that discipline. His primary data base in regard to identifying the scope of modern psychology comprises the complete set of volumes of the *Annual Review of Psychology* since it first appeared in 1950. His reading of these volumes is reflected in the two chapters in which he discusses developments in psychology since 1950 (New Vistas I and II respectively). The first of these two chapters deals with developments in the life sciences whilst the second covers developments in cognitive science.

He extends, enormously, the coverage, both in time and space, of his earlier book *A Short History of British Psychology: 1840–1940* (Hearnshaw 1964). I have indicated, in the previous paragraph, how he tackles developments in research since 1950. He treats the origins of psychology in antiquity in a chapter on the Greek philosophers and he deals with significant developments during the Middle Ages in a chapter on Christian theologians. There then follows an excellent trilogy of chapters on the scientific revolution, the philosophical renaissance, and eighteenth-century developments. These three chapters, together with the chapter on the life sciences referred to in the previous paragraph, form a prelude to a discussion, in chapter nine, of the metamorphosis of psychology, in the latter half of the nineteenth century, 'from speculative philosophy to scientific discipline' (p. 2). Apart from three very brief chapters – an introductory one, one on animism and a final chapter on metapsychology – there is only one chapter of any substance that has not already been mentioned. This deals with the history of applied psychology and with the fragmentation of the discipline that resulted from the development of specialized research, both pure and applied.

The whole volume is a highly scholarly production with more than a hundred pages of notes, references, and bibliographical material at the back. The author helpfully provides English translations of the various quotations in Latin and Greek that appear, from time to time, in the body of the text. It is a scholarly book in an age when scholars in psychology are rare. The reader will find between its covers the distilled wisdom of a lifetime of patient teaching and scholarship. Hearnshaw offers the introductory student a synoptic view of modern psychology set within a historical perspective that stretches 'from the dawn of civilisation to the present day' (publisher's blurb).

Scattered throughout the text is a series of literary vignettes of key figures who have helped to shape the development of modern psychology. Each is often accorded some five or six pages of text. There will be few surprises that the following qualify for this honoured treatment – Plato, Aristotle,

Augustine, Aquinas, Descartes, Locke, Kant, Fechner, Helmholtz, Wundt, James, Freud, and Piaget. More interesting, perhaps, is the inclusion of Bacon, Hobbes, Spinoza, Leibnitz, Vico, Marx, and Stern. It is a delight to see Leibnitz and Spinoza, in the seventeenth century, and Vico, in the eighteenth century, receiving serious scholarly attention in the context of a history of psychology. Minor figures who qualify for some two or three pages of text include Socrates, Galileo, Rousseau, Lloyd-Morgan, Darwin, Durkheim, Max Weber, Talcott Parsons, Pavlov, Skinner, and Chomsky.

Even minor figures are often portrayed in a highly graphic manner. Skinner, for example, is described as 'in the fullest sense of the word an "original" – a quixotic original, not without a beguiling quality' (p. 219). He elaborates (pps 286 *et seq.*) on Beloff's characterization of Chomsky as possessing 'a brilliant, but essentially medieval mind, [that has] somehow strayed into the computer age' (Beloff 1973). He describes Piaget as 'in some ways . . . his own worst enemy. He has been a compulsive and untidy writer, often abstract and obscure, and endlessly repetitive' (p. 278). Of James he says that 'in psychology he was a transitional figure, but a transitional figure of enormous importance, whose wide-ranging ideas could not be confined within the pre-occupations and limitations of the early experimentalists' (p. 144). Of Helmholtz he says that 'this hard-headed scientist was one of the most brilliant of psychological introspectionists' (p. 131). Fechner is described as 'a strange blend of physicist, philosopher, aesthetician, mystic and "inadvertent" psychologist' (p. 127).

Professor Hearnshaw's overall perspective is an eminently reasonable one. It is that psychology became a science in the latter half of the nineteenth century largely as a result of significant advances in the life sciences and the application of these successful techniques of research to the problems of philosophy. It is, however, a problematic science 'in that it is unavoidably reflexive' (p. 5). If psychologists adopt, as their model of science, the natural sciences then this is likely to result in an impoverishment in the subject-matter of psychology. Hearnshaw believes that this happened in the heyday of behaviourism. From his comprehensive and sympathetic outline of cognitive science in New Vistas II (chapter fifteen) one can infer that he is similarly apprehensive today, concerning the wisdom of adopting information technology as the model for psychological science. He favours a methodological pluralism within an overall conception of psychology as a science. He believes that 'hope for the future is closely linked with an appreciation of the past' (p. 6). He respects the rights of philosophers to be critical and sceptical of much scientific practice in psychology. This is clear in his chapter on philosophical critiques. He regrets that, by mid-century, the number of psychologists with a formal training in philosophy had dramatically diminished. He mentions the recent critiques of Gergen and of Harré concerning the scientific status of psychology. One senses that he is not entirely sympathetic to their particular point of view. Hearnshaw favours the argument 'that scientific methodology has been conceived too narrowly, that it can be expanded, without abandoning the Popperian schema of conjecture and refutation, to cope with the special features of psychology' (p. 5). Hearnshaw clearly favours 'boldness of imagination within the context of science' over 'revolutionary despair in the garments of philosophy' (p. 5). In this final chapter, which is a plea for the value of metapsychology, he nostalgically recalls the synoptic views of William Stern.

My main quibble with Hearnshaw's whole approach is that whilst he clearly acknowledges the reflexive nature of psychological science he is completely unselfconscious concerning the actual craft of the historian. Apart from his use of the *Annual Review of Psychology* as a major source of information, in regard to developments in psychology since 1950, he says little or nothing concerning the sources of his own understanding of history. He fails to discuss, for example, the status of Boring's classic study, *A History of Experimental Psychology* (Boring 1929/1950). At times he cites it as being authoritative. Yet he is also aware that its accuracy is problematic, as the following quotations will reveal: 'whereas Titchener and Boring and the older commentators stress the empirical and scientific aspects of Wundt's work, more recent studies have emphasised the idealistic and humanist components' (p. 135); 'the narrow travesty of Wundtianism represented in America by Titchener' (p. 213); and 'historians of psychology may have distorted Wundt's viewpoint beyond acceptable limits by ignoring the Leibnitzian features' (p.136). The latter quotation is the only point in the book that I could discover where Hearnshaw actually concedes that historians may distort the record. The controversy, however, concerning the accuracy of Boring's account is not brought out into the open and discussed as an interesting problem in its own right.

Danziger's powerful thesis concerning the positivist repudiation of Wundt (Danziger 1979), is cited, merely, as one reference amongst others in a footnote (footnote 65, p. 330). There is no reference to it in the bibliography nor is it discussed as an important thesis in the body of the text. Yet it is highly germane to Hearnshaw's own approach to the history of psychology. The centrepiece of Hearnshaw's account is the emergence of psychology as a scientific discipline in the latter half of the nineteenth century in Germany. The whole book is about the antecedents and consequences of this important transition 'from speculative philosophy to scientific discipline' (p. 2), i.e. the transition, in Comteian terms, from metaphysics to science. One important consequence concerns changes in the nature of the historical record. As Danziger points out, history is written by the victors and so the vanquished receive rather a raw deal at the bar of history. The victors, in this particular instance, were the positivists, i.e. the behaviourists. Committed anti-positivists, like Wundt, were vulnerable to their work being seriously misinterpreted and distorted by positivist historians of science. This is the essence of Danziger's thesis.

Positivism, however, can lead to distortions of a different kind in the writing of historical accounts. G. W. Allport (1954), for example, identified Auguste Comte as the 'founding father' of social psychology. This is not mentioned in Hearnshaw's treatment of the history of the social sciences (chapter eleven). Samelson (1974) accused G. W. Allport of creating a false origin myth for the discipline by selecting Comte as its ancestor. Comte, of course, was the father of positivism. By his choice of ancestor Allport was implicitly expressing his approval of certain 'positivist' developments in North American social psychology e.g. the behaviouristically oriented textbook of *Social Psychology* which his brother F. H. Allport had published in 1924. Samelson showed that G. W. Allport could not have been fully conversant with the works of Comte or else he would not have made the particular claim for him that he did. He then went on to identify the secondary, English-language source from which Allport obtained his information about Comte.

This error, on Allport's part, is an example of a particular fallacy which the historian Butterfield (1951) called the Whig fallacy in the interpretation of history. This refers to 'the tendency in many historians to write on the side of Protestants and Whigs, to praise revolutions provided they have been successful, to emphasize certain principles of progress in the past and to produce a story which is the ratification if not the glorification of the present' (Butterfield 1951: v). Butterfield, as a professional historian, is much more self-reflexive about the craft of the historian than is Hearnshaw. It would have been nice to see Hearnshaw discuss some of the sources of error and bias in the writing of historical accounts. I am sure his judicious assessments of the comparative merits of rival historical accounts of the same events would have made interesting reading. In the context of biography, Hearnshaw exercised his critical judgement, with devastating effect, when he identified the sources of error and bias in the work of the late Sir Cyril Burt (Hearnshaw 1979). Given the volume of current research in cognitive science on bias and heuristics and in social psychology on attribution theory it would be surprising if research psychologists could not, themselves, contribute, usefully, to debate amongst historians on sources of error and bias in historical accounts (Farr 1985).

Hearnshaw, clearly, had read Danziger's article on the positivist repudiation of Wundt, as he cited it in a footnote. It may be that he did not consider it to be an important article or, more likely perhaps, he only came across it when he had already completed his text and so he incorporated it, at a late stage, as a footnote. It is, however, a time bomb in relation to Hearnshaw's own approach to the history and philosophy of science. In his introductory chapter Hearnshaw laments the general lack of interest on the part of scientists, in the study of history. Paraphrasing a quotation from Bacon he says that 'The right road for the scientist is, in other words, not the study of history, but the active prosecution of research' (p. 1). The disinterest of scientists in history, however, is rarely as benign as this quotation suggests. They *actively* used history, I would suggest, for their own purposes. O'Donnell (1979), for example, has shown how Boring wrote his history, during the 20s, as a spirited and partisan defence of 'pure' research in experimental psychology at a time when there was a dramatic burgeoning of interest in the applications of psychology. O'Donnell showed how Boring used his professional involvement in the affairs of the American Psychological Association to promote, systematically, the cause of the 'pure' experimentalists and to impede the too rapid advance of the applied psychologists. This was the context in which Boring came to use history to legitimize his own particular, and highly partisan, view of experimental psychology and to prove to his philosophical colleagues, at Harvard, that the time was now ripe for psychology to escape from being under the tutelage of that discipline. O'Donnell writes as a historian and not as a psychologist. The positivists' repudiation of Wundt, as outlined by Danziger, was rooted in their own philosophy of science. Their commitment to science actually distorted their understanding of the past. They were far from being neutral in their treatment of history. The contemporary reappraisals of Wundt may now be due, in part, to the demise of behaviourism as the dominant paradigm for research in psychology.

What is exciting, today, about the history of psychology is the increasing number of young historians who are now writing about it. This is a generation of writers who do not feature in Hearnshaw's volume. They are not so susceptible to the sources of error and bias identified above. Indeed they have a vital role to play in correcting the excesses of purely 'internalist' accounts of the development of psychology. I have already referred, above, to one aspect of the work of O'Donnell (1979). His doctoral dissertation at the University of Pennsylvania was concerned with the origins of behaviourism in American psychology between 1870 and 1920 (O'Donnell 1985). Amongst other things he identified popular interest in phrenology as an important factor which significantly accelerated the spread and adoption of behaviourism in North America. I doubt if a positivist historian of psychology, writing an internalist account, would have identified this as an important factor. Mitchell Ash (1982), in his wonderfully detailed thesis on the history, up to 1920, of the Berlin School of Gestalt Psychologists, showed how they developed their own highly distinctive philosophy of science in the context of German science at the turn of the century. Ash's study was a doctoral dissertation, in history, at Harvard. The Gestalt psychologists are not accorded a particularly important role in Hearnshaw's history. In my own estimation, however, social psychology became an important precursor of cognitive science when the Gestalt psychologists, after their relocation in North America, found themselves in significant opposition to behaviourism as the dominant model of psychological science (Farr, 1985, 1987). They represented the perspective of the actor; whilst the behaviourists represented the perspective of the observer. The two perspectives, *taken together*, are important if one is to achieve, as Hearnshaw strives to, a synoptic perspective on modern psychology.

Another historian, though not so young as either O'Donnell or Ash, writing on the history of psychology is Donald Fleming. In his article on the history of attitude (Fleming 1967) he identified Darwin as having made a significant contribution to research on the topic. This is a perfectly valid point that had escaped the attention of most social psychologists who have, more or less, appropriated the concept of attitude (see Farr 1980). Historians often perceive the significance of events in dramatically different ways to psychologists.

For the professional historian the history of institutions is just as important as the history of disciplines. Hearnshaw pays only lip service to this particular point of view. His history, however, is written very much within the tradition of a history of ideas. In the opening two paragraphs of his chapter on the beginnings, in Germany, of scientific psychology he mentions the importance of the institutional setting. Yet there are no references to Ringer's classic study of *The Decline of the German Mandarins: the German academic community, 1890–1933* (Ringer 1969). Nor does he draw on contemporary evidence concerning the nature of Wundt's laboratory, e.g. the historian Michael Sokal (1981) has edited the journal and letters of James McKeen Cattell from Germany and England between 1880 and 1888. The work of Ringer has had an important influence on the work of the younger generation of historians like Ash and O'Donnell. I mention these various historians because Hearnshaw makes no references to their work in his own study. This is a pity, because historians have a great deal to contribute to our understanding of the history of psychology. I hope, when he comes to revise his book for a second edition, that he will include references to such work. Hearnshaw's book will be an invaluable aid to the teacher; it will be less useful, however, as a guide to those researching the history of psychology.

The range and scope of the study are impressive; the connections between the separate chapters much less so. The inclusion of a chapter on the Australian Aborigines and New Zealand Maoris is striking and interesting. Yet he fails to link this chapter, which is concerned with the dawn of civilization, with an account of the major publications concerning the Australian Aborigines that appeared in Europe in 1912–13, from the pens of such writers as Malinowski, Radcliffe-Brown, Durkheim, Freud, and Wundt. Yet he does deal with all these writers, except Radcliffe-Brown, in later chapters. He fails to see the influence of Wundt on the development of social sciences other than psychology. He is plain wrong when he states that 'some schools of psychology, like the psychoanalytic, had never taken much notice of Wundt' (p. 213). Freud wrote *Totem and Taboo* in order to refute Wundt's account (in his *Volkerpsychologie*) of the totemic age. Wundt's insistence that experimental psychology was concerned with the analysis of consciousness forced Freud to describe his own system as being a meta-psychology because he was concerned primarily with the unconscious. Freud's rejection of experimental evidence for repression was almost certainly linked to his *acceptance* of the Leipzig model of experimental psychology, i.e. one could not, by means of introspection, obtain evidence relating to repression, which was an unconscious mechanism. Hearnshaw does link his excellent exposition of Spinoza's philosophy with the subsequent development of psychoanalysis but fails to identify the influence of Spinoza on the development of Heider's social psychology.

Hearnshaw treats the life sciences in quite a lot of detail – both as a prelude to the emergence of psychology as a science (chapter eight) and in terms of significant developments since 1950 (chapter fourteen). It is nice to see his discussion of the work of Lloyd Morgan in the chapter on the beginnings of scientific psychology (chapter nine). Hearnshaw believes that Morgan's work 'has been unduly neglected in the standard histories of psychology' (p. 141). Boakes's (1984) carefully researched and beautifully illustrated book *From Darwin to Behaviourism* may have come out too late for Hearnshaw to take account of it. It does, however, deal with developments in the life sciences in an imaginative way and helps to correct some of the deficiencies to which Hearnshaw points. It would also have been nice to see Hearnshaw make some reference to Forrest's study of Galton (Forrest 1974). Given the immense erudition that Hearnshaw does display, it may seem churlish to quibble about a few omissions. It is reassuring, however, to know that there are other British scholars working in the field of historical research. It is interesting to note that some social psychologists are even beginning to write on historial themes. Festinger's study of the pre-history of man – *The Human Legacy* (Festinger 1983) – should qualify for mention in any future chapter on the dawn of civilization and Mike Billig's recent book on the sophists – *Arguing and Thinking* (Billig 1987) may serve to dent Hearnshaw's treatment of them, 'The Sophists themselves may have been embryo practical psychologists, but they contributed very little to psychology as such' (p. 18).

Hearnshaw is acutely aware that psychology is not a unified science. This knowledge alone has prevented many lesser mortals from even attempting to put it in some sort of historical perspective. I am delighted that this knowledge did not prevent him from tackling the task.

London School of Economics

BIBLIOGRAPHY

Allport, F. H. (1924) *Social Psychology*, Boston, Mass.: Houghton-Mifflin.

Allport, G. W. (1954) 'The historical background of modern social psychology', in G. Lindzey (ed.) *Handbook of Social Psychology*, Vol. 1, Reading, Mass.: Addison Wesley, 3–56.

Ash, M. G. (1982) 'The emergence of Gestalt theory: experimental psychology in Germany, 1890–1920', PhD dissertation, University of Harvard, 1982, University Microfilms; order no. 8303408.

Beloff, J. (1973) *Psychological Sciences*, London: Crosby, Lockwood & Staples.

Billig, M. (1987) *Arguing and Thinking*, Cambridge: Cambridge University Press.

Boakes, R. (1984) *From Darwin to Behaviourism: Psychology and the minds of animals*, Cambridge: Cambridge University Press.

Boring, E. G. (1929/1950) *A History of Experimental Psychology*, New York: Century (2nd edn Appleton-Century Crofts).

Butterfield, H. (1951) *The Whig Interpretation of History*, London: Bell.

Danziger, K. (1979) 'The positivist repudiation of Wundt', *Journal of the History of the Behavioural Sciences* 15: 205–30.

Farr, R. M. (1980) 'On reading Darwin and discovering social psychology', in R. Gilmour and S. Duck (eds) *The Development of Social Psychology*, London: Academic Press, 111–36.

Farr, R. M. (1985) 'Some reflections on the historical development of psychology as an experimental and social science. An inaugural lecture', The London School of Economics & Political Science.

Farr, R. M. (1987) 'The science of mental life: a social psychological perspective', *Bulletin of the British Psychological Society* 40: 1–17.

Festinger, L. (1983) *The Human Legacy*, New York: Columbia University Press.

Fleming, D. (1967) 'Attitude: the history of a concept', *Perspectives in American History* 1: 287–365. Published by the Charles Warren Center for Studies in American History, Harvard University.

Forrest, D. W. (1974) *Francis Galton: The life and work of a Victorian genius*, London: Elek Books.

Hearnshaw, L. S. (1964) *A Short History of British Psychology: 1840–1940*, London: Methuen.

Hearnshaw, L. S. (1979) *Cyril Burt: Psychologist*, London: Hodder & Stoughton.

O'Donnell, J. M. (1979) 'The crisis of experimentation in the 1920s: E. G. Boring and his uses of history', *American Psychologist* 34: 289–95.

O'Donnell, J. M. (1985) *The Origins of Behaviourism: American Psychology, 1870–1920*, New York: New York University Press.

Ringer, F. (1969) *The Decline of the German Mandarins: the German academic community, 1890–1933*, Cambridge, Mass.: Harvard University Press.

Samelson, F. (1974) 'History, origin myth and ideology: 'Discovery' of social psychology', *Journal of the Theory of Social Behaviour* 4 (2): 217–31.

Sokal, M. M. (ed.) (1981) *An Education in Psychology: James McKeen Cattell's Journal and Letters from Germany and England: 1880–1888*, Cambridge, Mass.: MIT Press.

Reviews

Hans Belting (translated by Christopher S. Wood), *The End of the History of Art?*
London: University of Chicago Press, 1987; £13.50; xiii + 120 pp.

Provocative titles have a tendency to mask highly conventional theses. Thankfully this is not entirely the case with this book. For in these two short essays Professor Belting offers some mature reflection on the current crisis in art historical method, and proposes at least the germ of a possible solution. Indeed the declamatory nature of the title is reset in a suitably academic pose in the opening paragraph of the first essay:

> The title is meant to raise instead two further possibilities, namely, that contemporary art indeed manifests an awareness of a history of art but no longer carries it forward; and that the academic discipline of art history no longer disposes of a compelling model of historical treatment. (p. 3)

Here, in essence, the problem and the solution confronted in this essay are placed side by side. Professor Belting argues that the academic discipline of art history has reached a crisis precisely because the normative and teleological models of classical historians of art are no longer tenable. He suggests that further developments in research and scholarship should adopt, in part, the disruptive and open-ended methods of contemporary artists. That is to say, a creative history of art applying research to single themes and issues which exist independently of a universalizing theory or system.

The thesis is closely argued through an examination of the 'classical' historians of art, Vasari, Winckelmann, and Hegel. Vasari in particular is singled out as the figure who did most to turn the history of art into a specific theory of art. Hoisting the standard of classical beauty and making this the norm to which all succeeding art should aspire. In consequence the history of art itself became a discipline which judged aesthetic value and historical worthiness by this established standard. Professor Belting goes on to suggest that Winkelmann in his *History of the Art of Antiquity*, of 1764, extended this orthodoxy. Seeking out the nature of the antique in order to make this the model for art in his own time. Hence,

> as before, aesthetic criteria determine the format and logic of the art historical narrative. For Winkelmann, art history was still a sort of applied art criticism. (p. 9)

The history of art as a discipline, then, becomes bound to a paradigm which is prescriptive rather than descriptive or analytical. Where a shift does occur in this established method it is 'only at great cost' (p. 9). For Hegelian aesthetics by insisting on art's link to a broader *Weltanschauung* renders the history of art a function of the history of culture. Moreover, this latter history is itself, for Hegel, 'a transitory stage in the process of the spirits taking possession of the world' (p. 11). It follows that art must be a mechanical aspect of a universalizing ideal which is subject to teleological laws.

The subsequent history of the discipline, as Professor Belting describes it, consists of the progressive disassociation of the history of art from an overwhelming conception of art. Throughout the nineteenth century, art historical enquiry became increasingly obsessed with a sequential ordering of art works governed principally by a notion of a progressive development of formal and technical modes. Certainly the author cites exceptions to this method, most notably Alois Riegl and his follower Wilhelm Worringer, and indeed, very briefly, Ruskin. But this later history of art is generally consumed by the reductive category of formalism. In this manner Professor Belting arrives at the problem he had outlined in his preface to the two essays, this being that

> both the artist and the art historian have lost faith in a rational, teleological process of artistic history, a process to be carried out by the one and described by the other. (p. ix)

In effect he has described the crises of both art and art history in the 'postmodern' age.

Two criticisms need to be voiced at this point. This analysis, which is effectively a history of the history of art, is entirely perfunctory and lacks both depth and rigour. To be fair the author is aware of this fault and the second essay in the book, 'Vasari and his legacy', is designed to augment the brief historiography which instructs the argument in the title work. However, this second piece is only some twenty-eight pages long and can hardly be described as a thorough and systematic analysis. More fundamentally, the historiography lacks a method which might allow the author to discuss several key issues, e.g. the significant distinction between the methods of Vasari and Winkelmann, Winkelmann and Hegel, etc., and the underlying reasons for transitions between theories of art and histories of art. In part this omission can be excused on the grounds that the aim of this work is to introduce the reasons for the crisis in art history and some possible avenues for fruitful exploration. However, it does seem that the author has, by reducing these various figures to polemicists, created a very convenient paper tiger.

This criticism of Professor Belting's method should not imply hostility towards the ultimate aims of his essay, nor his suggestions for the future of art historical research. Given that this central theme is 'the emancipation from received models of the historical presentation of art' (p. ix) and that

> these models were for the most part varieties of stylistic history. They presented art as an autonomous system, to be evaluated by internal criteria. (pp. ix–x)

then few contemporary historians would contest the value, and necessity, of his project. It is all the more regrettable that his proposals for future research should, in the description afforded in his text, remain quite so ill-defined and vague.

In a section entitled 'Possible areas of art historical research' Professor Belting lists six areas where the discipline may be usefully expanded. The first of these, demanding the opening up of a dialogue between the human sciences, and the consequent breakdown of the notion of autonomous academic disciplines, is already a central feature of the 'new' art history. Indeed it was self-evidently, though never self-consciously, an aspect of the 'old' art history. In his second avenue, the author is careful to note that 'stylistic history cannot simply be replaced by social history' (p. 30); however, he insists that it is an absolute imperative to relate the work of art back to its context. This serves to introduce the third notion, the inclusion of 'reception aesthetics' into art historical enquiry. Since this idea is absolutely central to Professor Belting's model it is worth describing at some length. Here is the professor's own assessment of the method:

> Reception aesthetics sketches out historical sequences in which a work is bound not only to its original audience, and not only to previous art, but also to future artists or works. . . . In this way production and reception together effect the historical transformation of art. Above all this procedure brings the original beholder together with the contemporary beholder: the one as cause of the work, the other as source of the question posed to the work. . . . In this way the inquiry constantly finds new directions. (pp. 30–1)

Clearly such a model allows for important areas of empirical research to be undertaken. The historian can map out the determinants of the production of a work of art, decipher its multiple meanings in reference to the pertinent cultural climate, and reflexively consider his or her own role in relation to the analysis of the object. But just as clearly this is not in any sense an original or 'new' method. Historians have long been aware of the need to take into account their own cultural identity and the value-laden nature of the questions they pose. Thus far, Professor Belting's proposals are less 'new' avenues and possibilities than a classic case of old wine in new bottles.

More interesting, however, is the author's determination to introduce into art history a semblance of the 'deconstructionist' techniques of the 'post-modern' artist. Large areas of contemporary art take as a subject the nature, function, and dissemination of art as a product. A project which involves the examination of the image and its public reception, and the relationship of the image/object to the history of art and the contemporary world. Professor Belting suggests that

> the same possibilities are available to art-historical study, and can even foster a critical revision of its questions and theories. (p. 53)

This is the most radical dimension of the project Professor Belting proposes, though in truth it is neither a method nor a model, but remains, within this text, something like Eliot's conception of time, 'a perpetual possibility'. Together these two essays offer a suggestion which may well point to a richer, 'creative' history of art. The great danger remains that, in proposing an alliance with the project of postmodernism in art, art history too might collapse into the bizarre and often absurd relativism of contemporary art practice.

Tom Normand
University of St Andrews

Joan Busfield, *Managing Madness: Changing Ideas and Practice*
London: Hutchinson, 1986; hardback £25; 406 pp.

Joan Busfield's account of the concepts and policies that have structured British psychiatry, mainly during the eighteenth, nineteenth, and twentieth centuries, adds to the slowly growing body of literature in the social history of madness. Other titles in the genre range from 'classics' such as Kathleen Jones, *History of the Mental Health Services*, or William Parry-Jones, *The Trade in Lunacy*, to more recent accounts such as Andrew Scull, *Museums of Madness*, or Vieda Skultans, *The English Madness*. In common with these works, Busfield tends to avoid the sociology of medical knowledge, commenting largely on questions of policy, administration, and treatment, rather than on the development of disease categories themselves.

The book is divided into two parts. The first deals with 'Theoretical Issues', which include: models of medicine in psychiatry; conceptions of illness, (classifications of disorders and social epidemiology of patient populations); deviance, social control, and illness (discussions of Szasz, Laing, Sedgwick, and Scheff); and medicine and power (Illich, Freidson, Foucault, Navarro, Scull, and Ehrenrich and English). This somewhat hurried run-through of the contemporary sociology of medicine is followed by part two: 'Historical Developments'. This begins with the sixteenth century, as it was then that the foundations of the Poor Law were laid, which in turn provided the context for the first state provisions for lunatics in the nineteenth century. This was also the period in which the early stages of professionalization of medicine occurred, involving, of course, the persecution and exclusion of women healers as 'witches'. Busfield then considers the development of the first separate provisions for lunatics in the private madhouses of the seventeenth and eighteenth centuries. She describes how the end of the eighteenth century saw major changes in the social organization of insanity with moral management; the reform movement that culminated in the public asylum system after 1845; and the changing patient population – from largely private patients in madhouses to largely pauper lunatics in county asylums. Busfield then charts the transformation of the therapeutic optimism of moral management into pessimism, amidst the overcrowded, underfunded, austere asylums for the chronically insane in the later nineteenth century. Finally, she describes the hesitant and ultimately unsatisfactory progress from custodial care to community care during the twentieth century, placing this largely in the context of the break-up of the Poor Law, developments in psychiatric medicine, and changing government funding priorities. The main theoretical contribution of this discussion is to argue that, *pace* Scull, the fiscal crisis of the state was an obstacle to, rather than a reason for, the development of community care. However, it is also clear (pp. 346f) that Busfield and Scull mean different things by 'community care' anyway. The former means genuine support in the community, while the latter means a gloss for closing institutions, without any alternative provision.

It should be said, though, that this is now all fairly familiar terrain, described in very similar terms by Kathleen Jones and Andrew Scull. One potential innovation of *Managing Madness* is that it combines theoretical discussion of the sociological status of psychiatry with its historical development. However, in the substantial historical section of the book, one finds virtually no reference back to the earlier 'theoretical' discussion. Obvious sociological themes and concepts that might have informed the data, such as professionalization, medicalization, capitalism, and patriarchy, which appear to some limited extent in Scull's *Museums of Madness*, are not really developed by Busfield at all. This is a pity, because she makes a number of criticisms of the anti-psychiatry, 'Marxist functionalist' and 'professional power' models in her first section, but none of these is elaborated in the second section. Perhaps one of her weakest points here is the dismissal of Foucault in three pages (128–30) as an idealist who believed that 'the power of the medical profession exists in its ideas' (p. 129). Had Busfield taken the notion of a power/knowledge conjuncture more seriously, this might have opened up her text to the nuances of practices and strategies that have been productive of psychiatric knowledge during the past two centuries.

One is left feeling that she has an underlying sympathy for what she calls the 'liberal-scientific model' of psychiatry, but this is never made explicit enough to generate further discussion. Thus despite her own stated rationale, 'we . . . need to examine the historical origins of existing ideas and institutions. The current shape and character of psychiatry and of the mental health services . . . are as much a product of past needs, pressures and struggles as of present forces', one might be left in doubt as to the precise contribution of historical work. Her study does not really add anything in the way of documentary archive research to the already available literature, and indeed many of her statistical tables are reprinted from Parry-Jones and Scull. For example, the link between the Poor Law and nineteenth-century asylums is well attested, but it would be interesting to know what considerations, other than general reasons of finance, determined the selection of inmates from the workhouse for the asylum.

On a more positive note, Busfield is clearly dissatisfied with generalized historical explanations that invoke 'professionalization', or 'medicalization', as self-sufficient processes. She is not above arguing like this herself; for example, discussing the emergence of public asylums, she says, 'Enlightenment thought created a new sense of the human capacity to control nature and to deal with problems of sickness and ill-health' (p. 190). The Enlightenment also encouraged a scientific spirit, a new pattern of philanthropy, etc. On the whole, though, Busfield does offer more specific and grounded historical explanations, as in her account of community care, which locates its origin in changes in therapeutic ideas, the institution of direct welfare payments, the changing professional image of psychiatry, and the new therapeutic optimism of the 1940s and 1950s. What is missing here, though, is any attempt to theorize the social relations of psychiatry as a whole.

As a general textbook for social history or sociology of medicine students, *Managing Madness* will be useful, if to some extent a replication of some other literature in the field. It at least brings the reader up to date with the background to recent mental health legislation in Britain. It should also be used by clinical practitioners looking for a comprehensive history of their field, although they are unlikely to find their theoretical preconceptions seriously challenged.

Larry Ray
University of Lancaster

Krishan Kumar, *Utopia and Anti-Utopia in Modern Times*
Oxford: Basil Blackwell, 1987; £24.50; 506 pp.

Reading this wide-ranging and scholarly survey of utopias, ancient but mostly modern, I could not prevent myself from beginning to see utopia and anti-utopia throughout modern social thought. Indeed, a central claim of Kumar's is that utopia is a specifically modern phenomenon invented by Thomas More. The conflation of *eutopos* and *outopos* did not merely produce a new word that would amuse his contemporaries. According to Kumar he actually produced the thing itself. This is to contradict all who have previously assumed that works such as Plato's *Republic* were utopias on the same footing as the modern variants. Why this is so is explained in terms of an argument to the effect that More invented both a new literary form and a new conception of human possibilities. More seems to have transcended the rhetorical conventions of his own time by the novel act of fusing within one text the classical or conventional dialogue form with a discourse, a narrative fiction. Further, the tradition that More inaugurated differed from the tradition of framing 'ideal constitutions', as in Bodin or Hobbes, for example, in that it presented the ideal society as a going concern and not as a model with which we may compare the existing state of affairs. In following this line of argument through, a difficulty arises. In Kumar's view *the* modern utopia is socialism and the most influential form of socialism is Marxism. Now it is a well-known fact that the two founders of Marxism took great pains to make it clear that there was a fundamental distinction between 'utopian' and 'scientific' socialism. Marx refused to write 'recipes for the cookshops of the future' although, as Kumar interestingly points out, this did not prevent some of his immediate followers from doing so. In other words the problem here is to say just what the term 'utopia' is actually referring to. Kumar wants to say that there is a utopia to be found in, for example, the writings of Saint-Simon, Marx, and Engels even though none of them ever wrote a formal utopia. Now it seems to be perfectly reasonable to say, as many have, that there are utopian elements in the work of Marx but in doing so this seems to undermine the conventional account of a 'utopia' as a fully sketched-out plan for an ideal society.

'Utopia' as a concept may well be one of those much-discussed 'essentially contested concepts' that pervade the human sciences. Kumar himself side-steps the problem, if it is a problem, by referring to the Wittgensteinian notion of 'family resemblances'. By so doing he avoids the trap of looking for some 'essence' of utopia and asserts that 'by use and context shall we know our utopias'. Nevertheless, does there not have to be some notion of what resembles what? Or is this too 'essentialist'? I think that Kumar is essentially correct in the line that he takes although specialists on utopian literature may want to criticize him on various points of detail. In following the strategy that he does he is able to cover an enormous area and to have something interesting to say on every topic that he covers. The sceptically nominalist flexibility of his approach allows him to be not unduly worried by the admission that the line of demarcation that he has erected between the ancient and the modern utopia cannot, at all times, be maintained.

An interesting use of the idea of utopia is to look at America as another candidate for the title of *the* utopia. Certainly, from its discovery, the New World offered glimpses of both a lost utopian past and a possible utopian future. John Locke, to name one prominent figure, had stated that: 'In the beginning all the world was America.' The utopian idea flourished throughout the early history of American settlement and beyond. The current but by no means new, as Tocqueville records, wave of religious fundamentalism is merely a version of the American idea of utopia. Borrowing the term 'meta-utopia' from the American philosopher Nozick, Kumar points out how it was that in the nineteenth century America was the land of utopian communities. America can be regarded in this light as a land that created a 'framework for utopias'. America in the nineteenth century was the place in which utopian ideas were practised in a way that had not occurred before and has not occurred since. The curious fact that emerges from a consideration of nineteenth-century America is that it was nationally one large utopian experiment which, at the same time, allowed a plurality of individual utopias each to follow its own vision. It is interesting to note too that the utopian nature of life in America was a fact that impressed most contemporary European socialists.

Utopias are important because they reflect the societies in which they are created. This is not to propose some reductionist and causal thesis in the sociology of knowledge but merely to state the truism that utopian ideas grow within specific social environments and are imaginative responses to them. To attempt to say more or to be more 'precise' is probably to ask for trouble. Thus, as Kumar points out, when we examine the content of utopian ideas we can see quite clearly that they are the products of particular times and places. Although many might want to question the separation of the classical from the modern utopia there is one clear difference and that is the fact that from More onwards there is a new concern with equality, work, and science that is introduced into this form of discourse. There might even be a 'Protestant Ethic and the Spirit of Utopia' waiting to be written.

The development of modernity has been marked by the introduction of an interesting and radically new element: science. Is the modern idea of scientific knowledge itself inescapably utopian? Again this is an element of the modern utopia that seems to contradict what is usually assumed to be one of its central features. The modern idea of scientific knowledge is one of endless progress. As soon as science enters utopia it loses its static character. If a society is perfect why or, indeed, how, can it change? But as soon as a 'scientific utopia' is created do we not have something of a contradiction? Or is it only a contradiction from an 'essentialist' point of view?

It is here that socialism enters the scene. In Kumar's words, 'socialism was the nineteenth-century utopia, the truly modern utopia, *par excellence*'. The modernity of socialism as *our* utopia is captured clearly when we see that it is a product of the convergence of More's communism and Bacon's science that also continued the Enlightenment tradition of belief in reason and progress. The modern form of anti-utopia is itself unthinkable without the prior existence of socialism. If socialism is in decline as a utopia does this not imply that much more is at stake than merely the inability of socialist parties to win votes? Could this be the tip of an iceberg, a sign that something much more fundamental is at issue? What does the decline of utopia imply?

Many writers have commented upon the 'decline' of utopia in the contemporary world. There seems to be no shortage of utopian writing if measured in terms of literary output. But what does seem to be true is that the decline of socialism as a unifying utopia has left a void. Habermas, for example, has recently decried the loss, in modern welfare states, of the utopia of classical socialism and its replacement by a fragmented array of particular utopian subcultures such as those of ecology and feminism. His own idea of an ideal *kommunikationsgemeinschaft* is itself a utopia clearly intended to replace the utopia that we have lost.

Bound up with the 'decline' of utopia is the fact that, almost from its origins, the modern utopia has called forth its antithesis: the anti-utopia. Five chapters of this book are each discussions of modern utopias and anti-utopias. The two most widely read and influential of these are anti-utopias. Huxley's *Brave New World* and Orwell's *Nineteen Eighty-Four* are much more representative of the contemporary intellectual mood than are Bellamy's *Looking Backward* or Skinner's *Walden Two*. The 'disenchantment of the world' by 'science' that Max Weber spoke of seems to have had its effect here. Nevertheless, this is to simplify the story for, as Kumar shows, there is a complex interplay between utopian and anti-utopian elements in the thought of the most creative writers in these traditions.

Kumar ends his study with a quote from Karl Mannheim, still one of the most significant writers on the subject, to the effect that man (modern man? Western man?) without utopian visions would no longer be recognizable as man. Without the belief in progress, it would appear, utopian thought is dead. But one of the characteristics of avant-garde thought, at least during the last forty years, has been the systematic undermining of the belief in progress both moral and scientific. Utopias are important because they shed light upon a fundamental feature of the predicament of modernity. As Mannheim saw a long time ago, if the modern age is an age of ideology then it must also be an age of utopia. If the idea of the 'end of ideology' was itself an ideology it was not an ideology with the power and vision of those it claimed to supplant. Similarly, the waning of utopias may not be complete but there is no doubt that there has been a fragmentation of the utopian imagination. And so it is with anti-utopias. Kumar points out that there has been no anti-utopia since Orwell's that has captured the public imagination to anything like the same extent and become the centre of intellectual debate. Further, we must not underestimate the influence of the idea, expressed by philosophers such as Berlin and Popper in the past and now revived by Rorty, that the very attempt to achieve utopian ends under modern conditions rests upon an untenable denial of moral pluralism that is bound to produce disastrous consequences.

Utopias are paradoxical things. They are both necessary, if the social and political imagination is not to disappear completely, and by definition, impossible to achieve.

Peter Lassman
University of Birmingham

S. G. Shanker (ed.), *Philosophy in Britain Today*
Beckenham: Croom Helm, 1986; £18.95; 315 pp.

The idea behind this collection was a good one: to canvass a number of leading philosophers now working in Britain regarding current trends in and future prospects for the discipline here, asking them to supplement their remarks with some autobiographical material which might help to explain the attractions of the subject. I take it that the book was originally intended to be accessible to an educated lay audience, including prospective students of philosophy. Unfortunately, though a number of interesting items are to be found in the volume, the editor has failed to exercise the discipline needed to realize his initial objective. What we have, in consequence, is a hotchpotch of essays, some of which are pitched at a fairly elementary level while others presuppose much more expertise, and some of which contain substantial amounts of autobiography while others contain none. One might, further-more, question the editor's selection of authors as being somewhat unrep-resentative of the contemporary British scene. Karl Popper, Antony Flew, R. M. Hare, Stephan Körner and Czeslaw Lejewski – almost half of the contributors – are either emeritus professors or have retired from their British chairs and are now based abroad. Only three of the contributors, including the editor himself (a Canadian), are younger than fifty.

Two of the essays have appeared elsewhere and have been revised for this volume: Karl Popper's 'How I see philosophy' and a lengthy piece by Gordon Baker whose Greek title is translated for us in a footnote as 'Philosophy: simulacrum and form'. Popper's limpid prose and breadth of vision contrast rather favourably with Baker's convoluted, jargon-ridden, and polemical style. The two philosophers also differ, unsurprisingly, in their estimations of the value of Wittgenstein's later work. Baker eulogizes it, attacking what he sees as its scientistic opponents who draw their inspiration from Frege and Russell. By contrast, Popper writes: 'Wittgenstein . . . denied the existence of serious philosophical problems. . . . I can only say that if I had no serious philosophical problems and no hope of solving them, I should have no excuse for being a philosopher' (p. 202). Popper finds an ally for this estimation in Ernest Gellner who, in a piece entitled 'Three contemporary styles of philosophy', accuses Wittgenstein and 'his intellectual progeny' of promoting the 'grossly repellent' theory that the proper observation of linguistic custom dissolves all philosophical problems. But Gellner, now a Professor of Social Anthropology at Cambridge, is in any case generally quite scathing about modern academic philosophy, describing the current burgeoning of formal logical techniques as the new scholasticism, 'quiddity on wheels', and dismissing Rawlsian liberal democratic theory as 'mayflower casuistry'.

The best and worst contributions to the volume are, in my opinion, Crispin Wright's 'Theories of meaning and speakers' knowledge' and the editor's 'Computer vision or mechanist myopia?' respectively. Wright's essay does not make easy reading for anyone unversed in contemporary philosophical semantics, but he poses some penetrating challenges to the currently widespread notion that a competent speaker of a language must be ascribed an implicit or tacit knowledge of an axiomatized 'theory of meaning' for that language. Shanker's essay, a lengthy, disorganized, and turgid diatribe against the alleged philosophical confusions of most current researchers in the field of Artificial Intelligence, is no more easy to read, but by contrast does not in any measure repay the effort. This was a case of sheer self-indulgence on the editor's part, and the book would have been far better (and 53 pages slimmer) without it.

Amongst the pieces I have not so far mentioned are an interesting recapitulation of his distinctive philosophical views by Rom Harré ('Persons and powers'), a characteristically dry and succinct attack on moral descriptivism by R. M. Hare, a rather abstruse and abstract methodological essay on philosophical analysis by Stephan Körner, a highly technical and idiosyncratic disquisition on logic and ontology by Czeslaw Lejewski, and two quite revealing essays in intellectual autobiography by Renford Bambrough and Antony Flew. Altogether, as I say, something of a hotchpotch, failing on the whole to reflect a faithful image of the main currents of philosophical thought in Britain today. But that the editor is not entirely *au fait* with the present state of the subject in this country is, in any case, suggested by the breathtaking opening sentence of his preface, in which he writes: 'At a time when so much is undergoing a radical readjustment in Britain – a euphemism for socioeconomic decline – philosophy is experiencing an extraordinary growth.' With half a dozen university departments currently faced with closure, such 'growth' is extraordinary indeed!

E. J. Lowe
University of Durham

Carol Zisowitz Stearns and Peter N. Stearns, *Anger: The Struggle for Emotional Control in America's History*
London: University of Chicago Press, 1986; £21.25; 295 pp.

Carol and Peter Stearns bring their shared insights, historical and clinical, to this exploration of 'anger', attempting to assess its incidence, the forms of control directed towards it, and the social and historical contexts in which it has been differently seen and reacted to. Refusing abstract definitions, they say that anger is 'an emotion, biologically related to a "fight" response and usually aroused in a situation judged as antagonistic' (p. 15).

Their emphasis on emotion leads them to the technical term 'emotionology'. 'We call the conventions and standards by which Americans evaluated anger, and the institutions they developed to reflect these standards, *emotionology*.' And where is the evidence for this emotionology? Wherever norms and prescriptions for appropriate behaviour are set out; substantially, in the manuals of conduct referring to child behaviour, parental behaviour, school and workplace behaviour, that have come down to us through time and are still written; these valuable documents record expectations if not actualities. Reliance on such material, which emanates from particular classes and ethnic groups, implies a partial coverage of the field, a fact of which the authors are well aware: 'This study deals primarily with an emotionology produced by the Protestant middle classes, one widely preached to other groups but not necessarily so widely adopted' (p. 16).

Within these limits the authors draw fairly clear patterns from impressively complex sources. Warning against 'rigid Freudian or Eriksonian models', they read the premodern seventeenth- and eighteenth-century situation as displaying anger in plenty – between neighbours, over fences, between families, over wills, or whatever. What distinguishes it from the modern period is that there was less *concern* with anger, fewer standards against which it could be measured, and shame rather than guilt was the mode of control.

In a period of transition leading up to 1800, a new emotionology emerged. Puritan and Catholic religious ideas joined with the new market relationships of capitalism to insert imperatives of anger control into conceptions of personality. A succession of styles of control can be traced, the clearest being what the authors call 'the Victorian synthesis'.

> The Victorians had little tolerance for anger in marriage on the part of either sex and viewed that emotion as a threat to what they treasured most in the home. Angry people lost the ability to control themselves, and in a world perceived as already too much out of control, the Victorians could not forgive the introduction of chaos into the one retreat that remained. Angry people, both husbands and wives, existed, to be sure, but these were people of bad character. Good husbands and wives would raise good children, and in these children of proper character, anger would be almost excised. (p. 50)

The engaging clarity of these standards, underlaid, of course, by 'double standards' and different working-class styles, gives way to 'the American ambivalence' of the period 1860–1940.

In this ambivalent period anger became empirically visible and engaged the attention of social scientists. It gained some recognition as a positive driving force, provided it could be 'channelled', as into the boxing gloves that every middle-class boy was expected to possess. But the complexities of this time of Darwin and Social Darwinism, the rise of consumer gratification, and other cultural changes, dissolve the outlines of any single anger ideal. It does, however, seem that children were less likely to be physically abused, although differences between mothers and fathers in tolerating anger were sometimes compounded by differences between teachers and parents.

Clarity is much more available in their treatment of anger at work. Partly because the early literature of management is both profuse and crass.

Munsterberg and Taylor are easy targets, and the 'emotional baggage' of Mayo, whose small-town, middle-class background led him to see work disputes as akin to a nervous breakdown, is neatly pointed up. Personality tests for 'docility', and the idea of displaced anger that could be talked out, all led to the emergence of a 'cool managerial style'; a style that reached back into the home.

> Employers, by dealing sympathetically with worker anger regardless of cause, must relieve anxiety so that no worker would go home 'carrying with him a mind full of worries and bitterness' [citing Roethlisberger and Dickson, *Management and the Worker*]. The workplace became the center of an attack on all manifestations of serious anger. (p. 123)

The 'managerial style', once identified, can then be recognized as flowing over into 'the raising of cool kids', and again into 'fighting fair in marriage'. Child-rearing passed from Victorian conceptions of childish innocence, to recognition and channelling, and now into its post-1940 third stage where an attempt was made to 'manage anger out of effective existence' (p. 158). And although the expression of anger in marriage has come to be positively encouraged in some quarters, the Stearnses argue that control has always encased these tolerable outbursts.

Conclusions after a journey through history are never easy, and certainly the authors are wary of unidimensional explanations, psychoanalytic, political or otherwise. They have no hesitation in identifying trends towards greater control, and they are open to the possibility that this has implications for our conceptions of ourselves. Indeed, an anguished if not quite angry cry enters into two of their final statements:

> One of the most insidious features of the anger control campaign, certainly, has been its potentially paralyzing insistence that anger is an internal problem rather than a normal response to external stimulus. (p. 238)

> We need greater self-consciousness, among experts in various disciplines, of the interconnectedness between their advice or findings and a wider, ultimately political, context of behaviour. (p. 239)

There are more themes in this interesting book than can easily be presented in a short space, perhaps the most important being the home/work dichotomy which runs like a single thread through the material. When work was gradually removed from the home and new forms of industrial production were introduced, it conferred on the domestic scene a subordinate, compensatory function. The consequences for our conception of gender roles and our notions of family life were so significant that we cannot today be said to have found a satisfactory balance. For this reason, history is instructive if we know how to read it:

> Our specific concern, anger, is of interest in itself, to be sure, but we also argue that, in looking at the ways the Victorians dealt with that emotion, we can offer a new insight into their reactions to their entire experience and that this experience, generated by the central problem of the home/work dichotomy, has much in common with our own. (p. 37)

As for themes they did not address in their knowingly limited sampling, the two most fascinating might be the anger of those who suffered race and class oppression and were unable to write about it, let alone write a manual of proper conduct, and secondly the role of higher education, particularly in the natural sciences, as the supreme form of anger disqualification; except of course in the military academies where channelling runs fiercely on. Given the rare combination of skills brought to this important topic, I would have liked to see slightly more clinical exploration of the material, to counterbalance the thoroughness of the historical enquiry. Still, the authors have opened out, most impressively, an area of concern that threatens to become more, rather than less, important with the passage of time.

Ray Holland
University of London

Books received

This is a list of books received up to 31 July 1987.

ARCHARD, David, *Consciousness and the Unconscious (Problems of Modern European Thought series)*, London: Hutchinson, 1984, paper £5.50, 136 pp.

AVIS, Paul, *Foundations of Modern Historical Thought: From Machiavelli to Vico*, Beckenham: Croom Helm, 1986, £19.95, 179 pp.

BAILEY, Victor, *Delinquency and Citizenship: Reclaiming the Young Offender 1914–1948*, Oxford: Clarendon Press, 1987, £30.00, viii + 352 pp.

BAUMANN, Gerd (ed.), *The Written Word: Literacy in Transition*, Oxford: Clarendon Press, 1986, £25.00, x + 197 pp.

BEISER, Frederick C., *The Fate of Reason: German Philosophy from Kant to Fichte*, London: Harvard University Press, 1987, £23.95, xi + 395 pp.

BELTING, Hans, *The End of the History of Art?*, London: University of Chicago Press, 1987, £13.50, xiii + 120 pp.

BENVENUTO, B. and KENNEDY, R., *The Works of Jacques Lacan*, London: Free Association Books, 1986, £20.00, paper £7.95, 240 pp.

BERSANI, Leo, *The Freudian Body: Psychoanalysis and Art*, New York: Columbia University Press, 1986, $17.50, 126 pp.

BHASKAR, Roy, *Scientific Realism and Human Emancipation*, London: Verso, 1986, £29.95, paper £9.95, 308 pp.

BION, W. R., *The Long Week-End: Part of Life*, London: Free Association Books, 1987, paper £6.95, 288 pp.

BOLLAS, Christopher, *The Shadow of the Object: Psychoanalysis of the Unthought Known*, London: Free Association Books, 1987, £25.00, paper £9.95, 283 pp.

BRAUDY, Leo, *The Frenzy of Renown: Fame and its History*, Oxford: Oxford University Press, 1986, £22.50, xiii + 649 pp.

BRODY, Hugh, *Inishkillane: Change and Decline in the West of Ireland*, London: Faber & Faber, 1986, paper £4.95, xii + 226 pp.

BRODY, Hugh, *Maps and Dreams: A Journey into the Lives and Lands of the Beaver Indians of Northwest Canada*, London: Faber & Faber, 1986, paper £4.95, xxv + 294 pp.

BUSFIELD, Joan, *Managing Madness: Changing Ideas and Practice*, London: Hutchinson, 1986, £25.00, 406 pp.

BYNUM, W. F. and PORTER, R. (eds), *Medical Fringe and Medical Orthodoxy 1750–1850*, Beckenham: Croom Helm, 1986, £30.00, 274 pp.

CHASSEGUET-SMIRGEL, Janine, *Creativity and Perversion*, London: Free Association Books, 1985, paper £5.95, ix + 172 pp.

CHASSEGUET-SMIRGEL, J., *The Ego Ideal*, London: Free Association Books, 1985, £22.50, paper £9.95, xvi + 271 pp.

CHASSEGUET-SMIRGEL, J. and GRUNBERGER, B., *Freud or Reich? Psychoanalysis and Illusion*, London: Free Association Books, 1986, £20.00, paper £8.50, 252 pp.

COHEN, Anthony P. (ed.), *Symbolising Boundaries: Identity and Diversity in British Cultures*, Manchester: Manchester University Press, 1986, £25.00, x + 189 pp.

COHEN, I. Bernard, *Revolution in Science*, London: Harvard University Press, 1985, paper £7.95, xx + 711 pp.

COLEMAN, D. C., *History and the Economic Past: An Account of the Rise and Decline of Economic History in Britain*, Oxford: Clarendon Press, 1987, £17.50, 150 pp.

COWELL, David, *Steps Ahead: Practical Applications of Educational Psychology for Teachers and Parents*, Bognor Regis: Anchor Publications, 1986, £7.95, 258 pp.

DARNTON, Robert, *Mesmerism and the End of Enlightenment in France*, London: Harvard University Press, 1986, paper £6.75, xiii + 218 pp.

DAUDI, Philippe, *Power in the Organisation*, Oxford: Basil Blackwell, 1986, £27.50, vii + 338 pp.

DOUGLAS, Mary, *Risk Acceptability According to the Social Sciences*, London: Routledge & Kegan Paul, 1986, paper £7.95, 115 pp.

DOVAL, Len and HARRIS, Roger, *Empiricism, Explanation and Rationality*, London: Routledge & Kegan Paul, 1986, paper £7.95, xiii + 200 pp.

EASTHOPE, Antony, *What a Man's Gotta Do: The Masculine Myth in Popular Culture*, London: Paladin, 1986, paper £3.95, 180 pp.

EISENSTADT, S. N. (ed.), *Patterns of Modernity: Volume 1, The West*, London: Frances Pinter, 1987, £25.00, ix + 185 pp.

EISENSTADT, S. N. (ed.), *Patterns of Modernity: Volume II, Beyond the West*, London: Frances Pinter, 1987, £25.00, vii + 223 pp.

EMSLEY, Clive, *Crime and Society in England 1750–1900*, London: Longman, 1987, paper £6.95, vi + 257 pp.

FILDES, Valerie, *Breasts, Bottles and Babies: A History of Infant Feeding*, Edinburgh: Edinburgh University Press, 1986, £25.00, xxviii + 462 pp.

FULLER, John G., *The Ghost of 29 Megacycles*, London: Grafton Books, 1987, paper £2.95, 351 pp.

GADAMER, Hans-Georg, *Philosophical Apprenticeships*, London: MIT Press, 1985, paper £8.95, xviii + 198 pp.

GALLI, Rosemary E. and JONES, Jocelyn, *Guinea-Bissau: Politics, Economics and Society*, London: Frances Pinter, 1987, £22.50, paper £6.95, xvi + 217 pp.

GANE, Mike (ed.), *Towards a Critique of Foucault*, London: Routledge & Kegan Paul, 1986, paper £6.95, vii + 179 pp.

GARFINKEL, Harold (ed.), *Ethnomethodological Studies of Work*, London: Routledge & Kegan Paul, 1986, £25.00, viii + 196 pp.

GASCHE, Rodolphe, *The Tain of the Mirror: Derrida and the Philosophy of Reflection*, London: Harvard University Press, 1986, £22.25, viii + 348 pp.

GOULD, Stephen Jay, *Time's Arrow, Time's Cycle: Myth and Metaphor in the Discovery of Geological Time*, London: Harvard University Press, 1987, £14.50, xiii + 222 pp.

HAMILTON, David, *The Monkey Gland Affair*, London: Chatto & Windus, 1986, £11.95, xvi + 155 pp.

HARRÉ, Rom, *Varieties of Realism: A Rationale for the Natural Sciences*, Oxford: Basil Blackwell, 1986, £25.00, viii + 375 pp.

HARVEY, Lee, *Myths of the Chicago School of Sociology*, Aldershot: Gower, 1987, £23.50, vi + 350 pp.

HEARNSHAW, L. S., *The Shaping of Modern Psychology: An historical introduction*, London: Routledge & Kegan Paul, 1987, £19.95, viii + 423 pp.

HERMAN, Nini, *Why Psychotherapy?*, London: Free Association Books, 1987, paper £7.95, 165 pp.

HOLMANS, A. E., *Housing Policy in Britain*, Beckenham: Croom Helm, 1987, £29.95, 489 pp.

HOLTON, Robert J. and TURNER, Bryan S., *Talcott Parsons on Economy and Society*, London: Routledge & Kegan Paul, 1986, £25.00, vii + 276 pp.

JONES, Greta, *Social Hygiene in 20th Century Britain*, Beckenham: Croom Helm, 1986, £25.00, 180 pp.

JORDANOVA, Ludmilla (ed.), *Languages of Nature*, London: Free Association Books, 1986, paper £7.95, 351 pp.

KOHON, G. (ed.), *The British School of Psychoanalysis: The Independent Tradition*, London: Free Association Books, 1986, £25.00, paper £9.95, 448 pp.

KOLB, David, *The Critique of Pure Modernity: Hegel, Heidegger, and After*, London: University of Chicago Press, 1986, £19.95, xvii + 316 pp.

KONVITZ, Josef, *Cartography in France 1660–1848: Science, Engineering and Statecraft*, London: University of Chicago Press, 1987, £32.50, xx + 194 pp.

KOVEL, J., *Against the State of Nuclear Terror*, London: Free Association Books, 1986, paper £3.95, 240 pp.

KUMAR, Krishan, *Utopia and Anti-Utopia in Modern Times*, Oxford: Basil Blackwell, 1987, £24.50, 506 pp.

LAKI, Stanley L., *Science and Creation*, Edinburgh: Scottish Academic Press, 1987, paper £6.50, viii + 377 pp.

LAWSON, Hilary, *Reflexivity: The Post-Modern Predicament (Problems of Modern European Thought series)*, London: Hutchinson, 1985, paper £5.50, 132 pp.

LECERCLE, Jean-Jacques, *Philosophy Through the Looking-Glass: Language, Nonsense, Desire (Problems of Modern European Thought series)*, London: Hutchinson, 1985, paper £5.95, 206 pp.

LEVIDOW, Les (ed.), *Science as Politics*, London: Free Association Books, 1986, paper (no price), 180 pp.

LINDNER, R., *The Fifty-Minute Hour*, London: Free Association Books, 1987, paper £7.95, ix + 293 pp.

LOUDON, Irvine, *Medical Care and the General Practitioner 1750–1850*, Oxford: Clarendon Press, 1986, £30.00, xv + 354 pp.

MAGGS, Christopher (ed.), *Nursing History: The State of the Art*, Beckenham: Croom Helm, 1986, paper £10.95, 199 pp.

MANICAS, Peter T., *A History and Philosophy of the Social Sciences*, Oxford: Basil Blackwell, 1987, £29.50, vii + 354 pp.

MARGOLIS, Joseph, *Pragmatism Without Foundations: Reconciling Realism and Relativism*, Oxford: Basil Blackwell, 1986, £25.00, xix + 320 pp.

MASSON, Jeffrey Moussaieff (ed.), *The Complete Letters of Sigmund Freud to Wilhelm Fliess 1887–1904*, London: Harvard University Press, 1985, paper £7.50, xv + 505 pp.

MATTICK, Paul, Jr, *Social Knowledge: An Essay on the Nature and Limits of Social Science*, London: Hutchinson, 1986, £23.50, x + 127 pp.

McDOUGALL, J., *Theatres of the Mind: Illusion and Truth on the Psychoanalytic Stage*, London: Free Association Books, 1986, £25.00, paper £9.95, xi + 301 pp.

McNEIL, Maureen (ed.), *Gender and Expertise*, London: Free Association Books, 1987, paper £8.95, vi + 266 pp.

MELMAN, Yossi, *The Master Terrorist: The True Story Behind Abu Nidal*, London: Sidgwick & Jackson, 1987, £12.95, 232 pp.

MERQUIOR, J. G., *From Prague to Paris: A Critique of Structuralist and Post-Structuralist Thought*, London: Verso, 1986, £18.95, paper £6.95, xi + 286 pp.

MISHLER, Elliot G., *Research and Interviewing: Context and Narrative*, London: Harvard University Press, 1986, £16.95, xi + 189 pp.

MONAGHAN, James, *Grammar in the Construction of Texts*, London: Frances Pinter, 1987, £22.50, vii + 155 pp.

NÄGELE, Rainer, *Reading After Freud: Essays on Goethe, Hölderin, Habermas, Nietzsche, Brecht, Celan, and Freud*, New York: Columbia University Press, 1987, $29.00, 225 pp.

NEWMEYER, Frederick J., *The Politics of Linguistics*, London: University of Chicago Press, 1986, £21.25, vii + 171 pp.

PHILLIPS, E. D., *Aspects of Greek Medicine*, Beckenham: Croom Helm, 1987, £22.50, 240 pp.

PORTER, Roy and WEAR, Andrew (eds), *Problems and Methods in the History of Medicine*, Beckenham: Croom Helm, 1987, £30.00, ix + 262 pp.

RICHARDS, B. (ed.), *Capitalism and Infancy*, London: Free Association Books, 1984, paper £7.95, 232 pp.

SALLIS, John, *Spacings – of Reason and Imagination: In Texts of Kant, Fichte, Hegel*, London: University of Chicago Press, 1987, £19.95, paper £8.75, xvi + 177 pp.

SAMUELS, A. (ed.), *The Father: Contemporary Jungian Perspectives*, London: Free Association Books, 1985, £22.50, paper £8.95, 280 pp.

SANDERS, Alan J. K., *Mongolia: Politics, Economics and Society*, London: Frances Pinter, 1987, £22.50, paper £6.95, xxi + 179 pp.

SHANKER, S. G. (ed.), *Philosophy in Britain Today*, Beckenham: Croom Helm, 1986, £18.95, 315 pp.

SHARPES, D. K., *An Asian Enquiry: Religion and Culture from Israel to Borneo*, Bognor Regis: Anchor Publications, 1986, £8.95, viii + 192 pp.

SLEE, Peter R. H., *Learning and a Liberal Education: The Study of Modern History in the Universities of Oxford, Cambridge and Manchester, 1800–1914*, Manchester: Manchester University Press, 1986, £25.00, x + 181 pp.

SOPER, Kate, *Humanism and Anti-Humanism (Problems of Modern European Thought series)*, London: Hutchinson, 1986, paper £5.95, 159 pp.

STEARNS, Carol Zisowitz and STEARNS, Peter N., *Anger: The Struggle for Emotional Control in America's History*, London: University of Chicago Press, 1986, £21.25, 295 pp.

STIGLER, Stephen M., *The History of Statistics: The Measurement of Uncertainty Before 1900*, London: Harvard University Press, 1986, £21.25, xvi + 410 pp.

STURROCK, John, *Structuralism*, London: Paladin, 1986, paper £3.95, xiii + 190 pp.

SYMINGTON, N., *The Analytic Experience: Lectures from the Tavistock*, London: Free Association Books, 1986, paper £8.95, 347 pp.

TAUSSIG, Michael, *Shamanism, Colonialism, and the Wild Man: A Study in*

Terror and Healing, London: University of Chicago Press, 1987, £23.95, xix + 517 pp.

TÖGEL, Christfried, *Struktur und Dynamik Wissenschaftlicher Theorien*, Frankfurt am Main: Verlag Peter Lang, 1986, paper (no price), 282 pp.

UNGER, Roberto Mangabeira, *The Critical Legal Studies Movement*, London: Harvard University Press, 1986, £15.25, paper £6.75, 128 pp.

VEYNE, Paul (ed.), *A History of Private Life: Volume 1, From Pagan Rome to Byzantium*, London: Harvard University Press, 1987, £24.95, ix + 670 pp.

VYGOTSKY, Lev, *Thought and Language*, London: MIT Press, 1986, £27.50, paper £8.95, lvi + 287 pp.

WARNER, Malcolm (ed.), *Management Reforms in China*, London: Frances Pinter, 1987, £22.50, x + 240 pp.

WHIMSTER, Sam and LASH, Scott (eds), *Max Weber, Rationality and Modernity*, London: Allen & Unwin, 1987, £30.00, paper £12.95, xvii + 394 pp.

WHITE, Hayden, *The Content of the Form: Narrative Discourse and Historical Representation*, Baltimore: Johns Hopkins University Press, 1987, $18.80, xiii + 244 pp.

WHITEHEAD, Alfred North, *Science and the Modern World*, London: Free Association Books, 1985, paper £6.95, xxiii + 265 pp.

WILDEN, Anthony, *The Rules Are No Game: The Strategy of Communication*, London: Routledge & Kegan Paul, 1987, £25.00, xv + 432 pp.

WOODWARD, David (ed.), *Art and Cartography: Six Historical Essays*, London: University of Chicago Press, 1987, £51.95, xvi + 249 pp.

YOUNG, Robert M., *Darwin's Metaphor: Nature's Place in Victorian Culture*, Cambridge: Cambridge University Press, 1985, £30.00, paper £10.95, xvii + 341 pp.

R
Routledge Journals

Enclosed is a sample copy of the journal you requested. Please complete the form below and return it to: Michelle Swinge, Routledge, Promotions, 11 New Fetter Lane, London EC4P 4EE

NAME:...

ADDRESS:...

....

....

NAME OF JOURNAL:.......................................

Please tick as appropriate

· · · · ·   I would like to subscribe to the journal and enclose my cheque payable to
            Routledge Journals

            Please charge my Access/American Express/Visa/Eurocard

            Account No □□□□□□□□□□□□□□□□

                                                        Card Expiry Date.........

· · · · ·   I will not be subscribing to this journal

Comments:···

···

···

11 New Fetter Lane, London EC4P 4EE. Telephone: 01-583 9855

Contributors

STEPHEN BANN is Reader in Modern Cultural Studies in the Faculty of Humanities, University of Kent. In 1984 he published *The Clothing of Clio* (Cambridge University Press), and he is continuing to work on problems connected with the representation of history in the post-eighteenth-century period. His most recent publication is a translation (with Michael Metteer) of René Girard's *Things Hidden since the Foundation of the World* (Athlone and Stanford University Press, 1987).

J. G. MERQUIOR, PhD (LSE) is an essayist and diplomat, now serving as Brazilian ambassador to Mexico. He was a visiting professor at King's College, London. His English books include *Rousseau and Weber: two studies in the theory of legitimacy* (RKP, 1980), the Fontana Modern Masters *Foucault* (1985), *Western Marxism* (Paladin, 1986) and *From Prague to Paris: a critique of structuralist and post-structuralist thought* (Verso, 1986). He is currently writing a study on the nature and images of modern culture.

ANTHONY PAGDEN is a Lecturer in History at the University of Cambridge and a Fellow of King's College. He is the author of *The Fall of Natural Man* (Cambridge, 1982 and 1987) and the editor of *The Languages of Political Theory in Early Modern Europe* (Cambridge, 1987) and, with Nicholas Canny, of *Colonial Identity in the Atlantic World* (Princeton, 1987). He is currently writing a history of anthropology in the eighteenth and nineteenth centuries.

MICHAEL ANN HOLLY is Associate Professor and Chair of the Fine Arts Department at the University of Rochester in Rochester, New York. She is the author of *Panofsky and the Foundations of Art History* (Ithaca, Cornell University Press, 1984), and this past summer was director of the National Endowment for the Humanities Institute on 'Theory and Interpretation in the Visual Arts'.

NORMAN BRYSON is a Fellow of King's College, Cambridge. He is General Editor of *Cambridge New Art History* and the author of three books on painting: *Word and Image, Vision and Painting*, and *Tradition and Desire*.